The Unforgettable Advantage

The Unforgettable Advantage

How to Deliver Service They Remember

Jennard Rose

BEP

BUSINESS EXPERT PRESS

Leader in applied, concise business books

The Unforgettable Advantage:
How to Deliver Service They Remember

Cover design by Cassandra Kronstedt

Interior design by S4Carlisle Publishing Services, Chennai, India

First published in 2025 by
Business Expert Press, LLC
222 East 46th Street, New York, NY 10017
www.businessexpertpress.com

ISBN-13: 978-1-63742-8-900 (paperback)
ISBN-13: 978-1-63742-8-917 (e-book)

Marketing Collection

First edition: 2025

10 9 8 7 6 5 4 3 2 1

EU SAFETY REPRESENTATIVE
Mare Nostrum Group B.V.
Mauritskade 21D
1091 GC Amsterdam
The Netherlands
gpsr@mare-nostrum.co.uk

Description

Deliver service they'll never forget, and build a brand they'll never leave.

In *The Unforgettable Advantage: How to Deliver Service They Remember*, businesses in both business-to-business (B2B) and business-to-customer (B2C) sectors will discover how to turn everyday customer interactions into extraordinary experiences that build loyalty, boost retention, and grow lasting brand value.

This isn't a book of theory or success stories—it's the missing manual on execution. With practical, step-by-step guidance, it empowers front-line teams, managers, and leaders to deliver consistently exceptional service in the real world.

From emotional intelligence and meaningful customer connection to service recovery and culture-building, *The Unforgettable Advantage* serves as both a leadership playbook and a frontline training tool. It equips your team to create service that not only delights but stays with people.

Whether you're in retail, hospitality, health care, education, or professional services, this book gives you the tools to build a service culture that customers remember and recommend.

Because in today's market, good service is expected. Only unforgettable service sets you apart.

Contents

Reviewer Quote

"What is missing in the digital world we live in today, is human connection. The ability to read body language, capability to use Emotional Intelligence with interaction. The Unforgettable Advantage: How to Deliver Service They Remember *is a MUST read for any employee and organization who has a customer."*—**Craig Gooley, Multi-restaurant Owner and Business Coach**

Introduction: The Art and Power of Service

Introduction

The words "Thank you for your service" carry more weight than we often realize. They aren't just polite acknowledgments; they signify moments where someone has gone beyond expectations, leaving a lasting impact. In the business world, these words are the true measure of success. They reveal not just a satisfied customer but also a loyal advocate—someone who feels seen, heard, and valued. Yet, despite the profound effect of exceptional service, it remains one of the most overlooked, undertrained, and underestimated aspects of business success.

Throughout my career, I've heard these words spoken with deep sincerity. Each time, they reaffirm my belief that service is not just about a transaction—it is about an experience. It is the difference between a forgettable moment and one that stays with a customer for years. It is the key to transforming businesses, elevating brands, and fostering unwavering customer loyalty. And yet, so many businesses fail to recognize this truth, treating service as an afterthought instead of the driving force behind long-term success.

The Misconception of Service as a Transaction

Too often, businesses see service as merely a function of the job—something that needs to be done to complete a sale. They focus on efficiency, automation, and cutting costs, failing to understand that customers aren't just buying a product or service; they are investing in an experience. Every single interaction is an opportunity to leave an impression, to build a relationship, and to create something memorable.

Service is not about getting customers in and out as quickly as possible. It is not about scripted greetings, robotic interactions, or simply meeting basic expectations. It is about reading people, understanding their needs, and anticipating what they want before they even ask. It is about making people feel welcomed, valued, and important. Until businesses stop viewing service as just another aspect of operations and start recognizing it as the heart of their success, true transformation will remain out of reach.

Good service meets expectations. Unforgettable service exceeds them.

Think of a time when you had a truly outstanding customer service experience. What made it memorable? Chances are, it wasn't just that the product was good or that the staff were polite. It was something more—something that made you feel special, appreciated, and important. It was a human connection, a moment of genuine care, or a personalized touch that made all the difference.

Businesses that master this level of service don't just attract customers; they create loyal advocates. They build relationships that go beyond the transactional, forging emotional connections that keep people coming back, not just because they need something but because they enjoy the experience.

Service Is Not a Task—It Is an Art

One of the biggest mistakes businesses make is treating service like a checklist:

- Greet the customer.
- Take the order.
- Deliver the product.
- Say, "Have a nice day."

This is not service. This is going through the motions. True service is an art form—one that requires skill, intuition, and emotional intelligence. It is about reading a room, understanding body language, and responding to unspoken needs. It is about recognizing when a customer is in a hurry and adjusting your pace accordingly or sensing when someone needs a bit of extra attention and care.

The businesses that get this right are the ones that stand out in a crowded marketplace. They create environments where customers feel at home, where they don't just come to buy—they come to belong.

Who Is This Book For?

This book is for leaders, managers, and frontline professionals in both **B2B (business-to-business) and B2C (business-to-consumer)** environments who understand that service is the foundation of long-term success.

- **For B2B Professionals**: Whether you manage client accounts, work in sales, or lead service teams, this book will help you build deeper relationships, enhance customer retention, and position your business as an indispensable partner.
- **For B2C Businesses**: Whether you run a café, retail store, or service-driven company, these strategies will help you create experiences that turn one-time buyers into lifelong customers.

No matter your industry, this book will give you the tools to move beyond transactions and create lasting, meaningful connections that drive loyalty and long-term success.

Why Service Should Be a Business's Top Priority

In today's competitive market, customers have endless choices. If they don't feel valued at one business, they can easily take their money elsewhere. Customers have a choice. You, at that moment of service, are their choice. Your desire is to be the only choice the customer will make. The businesses that thrive are the ones that understand that service is not just a part of the business—it is the business.

Prioritizing service means:

- Increased customer loyalty
- Higher customer retention rates
- More positive word-of-mouth and referrals
- Greater employee satisfaction and engagement
- Stronger brand reputation

Many businesses spend enormous amounts of money on marketing, advertising, and promotions, trying to attract new customers. But what if they simply provided such incredible service that their customers never left? What if their service was so outstanding that their customers couldn't stop talking about them? That kind of organic loyalty is more powerful than any advertising campaign.

On the flipside, poor service is one of the quickest ways to destroy a business. Studies show that customers are far more likely to share bad experiences than good ones. In the age of online reviews and social media, one bad experience can be broadcast to thousands of potential customers in an instant.

Consider this:

- A significant portion of customers who have a bad experience won't return.
- Many customers are willing to pay extra for a superior customer experience.
- Just one negative review can deter numerous potential customers.

No business can afford to ignore the power of service. And yet, many still do, thinking that price, convenience, or product selection alone will keep them competitive. But customers today expect more—they expect to be treated with respect, care, and appreciation. The businesses that understand this are the ones that will dominate their industries.

Why This Book Matters

This book is not just about service—it's about changing the way we think about service for our customers. It is about shifting from a transactional mindset to a practical one. It is about understanding that the businesses that master service will always have the upper hand over those that don't.

Whether you are a business owner, a manager, or a frontline employee, this book will provide you with the tools, strategies, and mindset needed to elevate your service to world-class levels. You will learn how to:

- Read a room and anticipate customer needs before they arise.
- Turn ordinary interactions into unforgettable moments.
- Create a welcoming atmosphere that customers don't want to leave.

- Build long-term relationships that drive repeat business.
- Lead and train teams to prioritize service at every level.

This book is a call to action—a call for businesses to stop treating service as an afterthought and start seeing it as the single most powerful tool for growth, success, and longevity.

The service industry is evolving. As the cost of living rises, so do customer expectations. People are becoming more selective about where they spend their money, and they expect more in return. Businesses that fail to meet these expectations will struggle to survive. But those who embrace this shift—those who go above and beyond to create experiences, not just transactions—will thrive.

If you are ready to elevate your business, redefine your approach to service, and create experiences that keep customers coming back, then this book is for you.

Together, let's build a future where exceptional service is the standard, where businesses don't just serve customers but create loyal supporters for life.

Let's begin.

PART 1

First Impressions and Customer Connection

A first impression is not just an introduction; it's a promise. The way you connect in those first moments determines whether a customer feels like a transaction or a valued guest.

CHAPTER 1

First Impressions: The 15-Second Rule and the Power of a Smile

I once worked for a company I loved—not just for their products or reputation but because they shared my passion for people and service. One of the core principles they taught me—and one I carry with me to this day—is the importance of the first 15 seconds. Wow them in 15.

Those first 15 seconds are a critical window of opportunity. In that brief moment, you can create a positive, lasting impression that sets the tone for the entire experience. Whether you're greeting a customer, starting a business meeting, or welcoming a guest into your home, the first 15 seconds can make or break the interaction.

We all know the saying, "You never get a second chance to make a first impression." But the power of those initial moments goes far beyond clichés. It's not just about looking the part or delivering a rehearsed greeting. It's about being intentional, authentic, and present in a way that resonates with the person in front of you. The first few moments of a customer's interaction with a business are critical. In that brief window, people unconsciously evaluate everything from the tone of a greeting to the cleanliness of the environment and begin forming lasting opinions. This all happens in our subconscious without us even knowing. This early assessment often determines whether they feel welcomed, valued, and inclined to return. While these impressions happen quickly, their impact can shape the entire customer experience and heavily influence long-term loyalty.

The Psychology Behind First Impressions

Why do those 15 seconds matter so much? Science has the answer. Studies show that humans form judgments about people, places, and experiences within milliseconds. These judgments are based on visual cues like body language, facial expressions, and grooming, as well as auditory cues like tone of voice and word choice.

Once an impression is formed, it's hard to change. If the first 15 seconds of an interaction feel cold, disorganized, or inattentive, it takes significantly more effort to turn things around. On the other hand, if those moments are warm, inviting, and intentional, you've set a strong foundation for trust and connection.

The 15-Second Rule Across Industries

No matter what field you work in, the principle of the first 15 seconds applies. Let me walk you through some examples to illustrate just how transformative this concept can be.

Retail

Imagine walking into a boutique clothing store. As you step through the door, no one acknowledges you. You wander around for a few minutes, unsure where to start or whether anyone is available to help. How likely are you to make a purchase?

Now imagine a different scenario. As soon as you enter, a staff member greets you with a warm smile and says, "Welcome! Let me know if there's anything I can help you find today." That simple acknowledgment immediately makes you feel seen, valued, and more inclined to engage.

The first 15 seconds in retail can determine whether a customer stays or walks out. A warm greeting, eye contact, and approachable body language can turn a casual browser into a loyal customer.

Hospitality

In the hospitality industry, the first 15 seconds are even more pronounced. Think about checking into a hotel. If the receptionist barely looks up from their screen and mumbles a half-hearted "Checking in?" it sets a negative tone for your stay.

Contrast that with a receptionist who greets you by name (if pre-informed), offers a friendly smile, and says, "Welcome! We're so glad you're here. Let me take care of you." That interaction makes you feel like more than just a booking number—it makes you feel like a valued guest.

Health care

In health care, the stakes are often higher because emotions like anxiety and vulnerability are at play. Picture a patient walking into a doctor's office. If the receptionist doesn't make eye contact or greet them with a rushed, impersonal attitude, the patient may feel even more nervous.

On the other hand, a simple, empathetic acknowledgment like, "Good morning, how can I assist you today?" can put the patient at ease and create a sense of trust in the care they're about to receive.

Corporate Environments

Even in the corporate world, where interactions often feel transactional, the first 15 seconds matter. Imagine walking into a boardroom for a job interview. If the interviewer doesn't smile or shake your hand without making eye contact, you immediately sense a disconnect.

Now picture an interviewer who greets you warmly, introduces themselves, and makes an effort to create rapport. You feel more confident, relaxed, and ready to engage, simply because of how they made you feel in those first moments.

The Elements of a Strong First Impression

So, how can you make the most of those 15 seconds? Here are some key elements to focus on:

1. **Body Language**

   Your posture, gestures, and facial expressions speak volumes before you even open your mouth. Stand tall, maintain eye contact, and smile genuinely. These nonverbal cues communicate confidence, approachability, and respect.

2. **Tone of Voice**

   Your tone can convey warmth, enthusiasm, and sincerity—or the lack thereof. Speak clearly and with energy, but avoid coming across as overly rehearsed or artificial.

3. **Personalization**

   Whenever possible, personalize your greeting. Use the person's name if you know it, or tailor your approach based on the context. For example, "Good afternoon, how can I help you today?" feels much more engaging than a generic "Next!"

4. **Attentiveness**

   Show that you're fully present in the moment. Put away distractions, whether it's a phone, computer screen, or anything else that pulls your focus away from the interaction.

5. **Authenticity**

   People can sense when you're being genuine versus when you're going through the motions. Be yourself, and let your passion for what you do shine through.

Lessons from My Career

Over the years, I've seen the power of the first 15 seconds play out time and time again. When I worked at that company I loved, they drilled this concept into everything we did. Whether it was greeting customers, answering phones, or responding to inquiries, we treated every initial interaction as an opportunity to create a positive imprint.

One example that stands out is a time when a customer walked into the store looking visibly frustrated. Instead of ignoring their demeanor, I greeted them warmly and asked, "Is there anything I can do to make your day a little better?" That one question shifted their entire mood. They ended up sharing their frustrations, and I helped them find exactly what they needed. By the time they left, they were smiling and thanking me profusely.

How to Apply This Principle

Here are practical ways to incorporate the 15-second rule into your daily work:

- **Train Your Team:** Make the first 15 seconds a cornerstone of your customer service training. Role-play scenarios to help your team practice making strong initial connections.
- **Audit Your Space:** Look at your business through the eyes of a first-time visitor. Is the environment welcoming? Are your staff approachable?
- **Lead by Example:** As a leader, demonstrate the importance of first impressions by embodying these principles in your own interactions.

The first 15 seconds are more than just a moment—they're a mindset. They remind us that every interaction, no matter how small, carries the potential to create something extraordinary.

If you commit to making those 15 seconds count, you'll not only elevate your own performance but also inspire those around you to do the same. Together, we can create experiences that leave people feeling seen, valued, and deeply connected.

The Power of a Smile

A smile is one of the simplest, most universal ways to connect with others. It transcends language barriers, cultural differences, and even bad days. Yet, it is often underestimated in its power to transform interactions, relationships, and experiences.

I've seen the incredible impact a smile can have throughout my career. Whether it was turning around a customer's day, building trust with a colleague, or creating an inviting environment, the act of smiling became a cornerstone of how I approached service and leadership. This part is dedicated to understanding why a smile matters, how it influences others, and how we can practice incorporating it into our daily lives and work.

Why Does a Smile Matter?

The answer lies in neuroscience.

When we see someone smile, our brains instinctively respond, often triggering a mirrored emotional reaction that helps build connection and warmth. This neurological response explains why seeing a genuine smile often prompts us to smile back, creating an instant sense of connection. In customer interactions, this means that a well-placed smile can set the tone for a positive experience, influencing not just mood but also the likelihood of a customer returning.

A smile isn't just a polite gesture—it's an emotional catalyst. Studies have shown that customers perceive employees who smile as more competent, approachable, and trustworthy. In fact, an authentic smile can even soften the impact of minor service mistakes, making customers more forgiving.

From a scientific standpoint, smiles are hardwired into our biology. When we smile, our brains release feel-good chemicals like dopamine, endorphins, and serotonin. These natural mood boosters not only make us feel better but also signal positivity and approachability to others. Because smiles are contagious, they create a ripple effect of positivity that can uplift an entire room or workplace.

By making smiling a natural and consistent part of customer interactions, businesses can create an environment where positivity is contagious, leading to stronger relationships and greater customer loyalty.

Beyond science, the benefits of smiling extend to practical, everyday interactions:

1. **Break Down Barriers:** Intense or unfamiliar situations, a smile can dissolve unease and make others feel more comfortable.
2. **Build Trust:** People are more likely to trust someone who smiles genuinely, as it conveys warmth and sincerity.
3. **Enhance Communication:** A smile softens conversations and makes feedback, instructions, or even criticism easier to deliver and receive.
4. **Foster Loyalty:** Customers, clients, and team members are more likely to remain loyal to businesses and leaders who create a welcoming, positive environment.

The Smile in Action: Real-Life Examples

Let me share some moments where a smile changed everything:

In Retail:

A woman once walked into the store I managed, looking visibly upset. My instinctive response was to greet her with a warm, genuine smile and say, "It's great to see you today! How can I help?" She immediately softened and began sharing her concerns. By the time she left, she was laughing and thanking me not only for solving her issue but also for making her feel better.

In Leadership:

During a particularly tough meeting with my team, emotions were running high. I noticed the tension and decided to shift my tone, beginning with a smile and saying, "Let's take a deep breath and figure this out together." That small gesture broke the ice, and the conversation became collaborative instead of confrontational.

In Customer Service:

One of my most memorable experiences involved a customer who was furious about a mistake with their order. Instead of mirroring their frustration, I smiled, apologized sincerely, and reassured them that I would make it right. By the end of the interaction, they were not only satisfied but in fact left a glowing review about how well the situation was handled.

The Impact of a Smile Across Industries

The power of a smile isn't confined to one field—it's universally impactful.

Health care

Imagine a nurse walking into a patient's room with a warm smile. That simple act can ease anxiety and create a sense of trust, even before a word is spoken. Studies show that patients rate their care more positively when health care providers smile and display compassion.

Hospitality

In hotels, restaurants, and other service-based industries, a smile is often the first impression. It sets the tone for the guest's experience and determines whether they feel welcome or like just another transaction.

Education

For teachers, smiling can create a more inviting learning environment. A welcoming smile can help students feel safe, encouraged, and more willing to participate.

Corporate Settings

In business, smiling during meetings or presentations can make you appear more confident and approachable. It fosters collaboration and helps build stronger professional relationships.

Practicing the Art of Smiling

Smiling may seem like an instinctive act, but it's also a skill that can be cultivated. Here are ways to practice smiling more intentionally:

1. **Start with Self-Awareness**

   Pay attention to your facial expressions throughout the day. Are you frowning or looking neutral even when you're not upset? Becoming aware of your default expression is the first step toward changing it.

2. **Practice Genuine Smiling**

   A genuine smile engages the muscles around your eyes, not just your mouth. Practice smiling in front of a mirror to recognize what a natural, authentic smile feels like.

3. **Use Visual Triggers**

   Place reminders in your environment to smile—whether it's a sticky note on your desk or a positive affirmation on your phone screen.

4. **Engage in Gratitude**

   Think of something that makes you happy or grateful before interacting with others. This will naturally bring a smile to your face.

5. **Role-Play Scenarios**

   During team training or personal development exercises, role-play scenarios where smiling could make a difference. For example, practice greeting customers or resolving conflicts with and without a smile, and note the difference in outcomes.

Overcoming Challenges to Smiling

While smiling is powerful, it's not always easy—especially when you're stressed, tired, or dealing with difficult situations. Here's how to overcome those challenges:

When You're Stressed
- Take a moment to breathe deeply and center yourself before engaging with others.
- Remind yourself that a smile can improve your mood and make the situation more manageable.

When It Feels Forced
- Focus on the person in front of you and their needs. A genuine connection often brings out a natural smile.
- If you can't manage a full smile, a slight upward curve of your lips can still convey positivity.

When It's Not Reciprocated
- Remember that your smile is about creating a positive atmosphere, not controlling others' reactions.
- Continue to smile, knowing that it can still influence the interaction, even if the response isn't immediate.

Building a Culture of Smiles

If you're a leader, you have the power to cultivate a workplace culture where smiling is a norm. Here's how:

1. **Lead by Example:** Smile often and encourage your team to do the same.
2. **Recognize Positivity:** Celebrate employees who create a welcoming atmosphere through their demeanor.
3. **Provide Training:** Teach the importance of smiling during customer interactions and team communication.

4. **Foster Joy:** Create an environment where employees feel valued, supported, and happy to be at work. This creates a real smile.

The impact of a smile doesn't end with the person you're interacting with. It creates a ripple effect that can extend to others. When you smile at a customer, they're more likely to smile at the next person they meet. When you smile at a colleague, it can improve their mood and productivity for the rest of the day.

In my experience, a workplace filled with genuine smiles is a workplace that thrives. Smiles build connections, foster loyalty, and make every interaction more meaningful.

Never underestimate the power of a smile. It's one of the simplest yet most profound ways to create a positive impact in the world around you. Start practicing today—smile at a stranger, a colleague, or a customer. Smile when things are going well, and especially when they're not.

If you commit to making a smile part of your daily life, you'll not only transform your interactions but also transform yourself and those around you.

CHAPTER 2

Creating Connection: Small Talk, Names, and Personalization

In the world of service, we often focus on the functional side of what we do: preparing meals, completing transactions, or delivering services. While these are essential elements, they are not what that set exceptional service apart. The real magic happens in the connections we create with people, and one of the simplest yet most powerful ways to build that connection is by changing the way we greet others.

Instead of a transactional "Good morning, how can I help you?" try saying, "Good morning, how are you?"

This small shift can create a ripple effect of positivity, loyalty, and trust. It's a question that invites engagement, shows genuine care, and transforms a routine interaction into a meaningful experience. Over the years, I've trained multiple hospitality crews to adopt this approach, and the results were remarkable—not just for the customers but also for the team and the business.

Why "How Are You?" Matters

Interpersonal emotion regulation refers to the process of managing one's own emotions and influencing the emotions of others during social interactions (Grandey et al. 2020). In the context of customer service, this concept is particularly important, as interactions often involve fluctuating emotions that need to be navigated effectively to maintain positive outcomes. Asking "How are you?" in a genuine, empathetic manner acknowledges and validates a customer's emotional state. More than a polite gesture, it can shape the tone of the entire interaction, helping to ease tension, build rapport, and create a sense of emotional safety that encourages trust. This practice helps ensure that both customers and employees maintain a constructive emotional experience, ultimately improving service quality and workplace culture.

At its core, "How are you?" is a question that recognizes the humanity in the other person. It signals that they are not just a customer, client, or colleague—they are a person whose feelings and experiences matter. Here's why this phrase is so impactful:

1. **Builds Personal Connections**

   Asking "How are you?" encourages a two-way interaction rather than a one-sided transaction. It's an opportunity to engage on a personal level, even if only briefly.

2. **Conveys Genuine Care**

   People can sense when you're being authentic. A heartfelt "How are you?" shows that you care about their well-being, not just their business.

3. **Encourages Loyalty**

   Customers remember how you made them feel. When they feel valued and seen, they're more likely to return and recommend your business to others.

4. **Enhances Team Morale**

   When team members greet each other with "How are you?" it fosters a culture of care and connection within the workplace, boosting morale and collaboration.

5. **Sets the Tone**

   "How are you?" is a warm, inviting way to start an interaction. It puts people at ease and opens the door for a positive experience.

Real-Life Transformations

I've seen firsthand how this small change can lead to extraordinary outcomes. Here are a few stories that illustrate the power of asking "How are you?"

Case Study 1: Turning Transactions into Relationships

At one café I managed, we trained the team to greet every customer with "Good morning, how are you today?" rather than the usual "What can

I get you?" The shift was almost immediate. Customers began sharing snippets of their day, from celebrations to challenges. Over time, these brief exchanges built relationships, and customers started coming back not just for the coffee but also for the connection.

Case Study 2: Resolving Customer Complaints

In another setting, a customer approached the counter visibly upset about a mistake with their order. Instead of diving into problem-solving, the team member began with saying, "I'm so sorry about that. How are you today?" The question diffused the customer's frustration and opened the door for a calm, productive resolution.

Case Study 3: Building Team Cohesion

I once trained a hospitality crew to greet each other with "How are you?" during shift changes. It fostered camaraderie and created a culture where team members felt supported and seen. This improved not only morale but also teamwork and service quality.

How to Ask "How Are You?" Effectively

While the phrase is simple, its delivery matters. Here's how to make it impactful:

1. **Be Genuine**
   People can tell when you're asking out of habit versus when you truly care. Make eye contact, use a warm tone, and be present in the moment.
2. **Listen to the Response**
   Asking "How are you?" is only meaningful if you listen to the answer. Whether the response is "I'm great, thank you!" or "I've had better days," acknowledge it with empathy.
3. **Tailor Your Interaction**
   If someone shares that they're having a rough day, a small gesture—like a kind word or extra effort—can make a big difference.

4. **Train Your Team**

Teach your team the importance of this approach and role-play scenarios to practice authentic greetings.

5. **Be Consistent**

Incorporate "How are you?" into every customer interaction, from greetings to goodbyes. Consistency reinforces its impact.

The Science Behind "How Are You?"

Research supports the power of personalized interactions. Studies show that people are more likely to form positive impressions of those who express genuine interest in them. Additionally, social connection is a fundamental human need. When we ask "How are you?" we're tapping into this need and creating a sense of belonging.

The Impact Across Industries

The "How are you?" approach isn't limited to hospitality—it's effective in every industry.

Retail

Greeting customers with "How are you?" creates a more personal shopping experience, leading to increased satisfaction and sales.

Health Care

Asking patients, "How are you feeling today?" builds trust and helps providers offer more compassionate care.

Education

Teachers who start their day by asking students, "How are you?" create a supportive, engaging learning environment.

Corporate Settings

In business, leaders who check in with their team members foster stronger relationships and improve workplace culture.

Challenges and Solutions

While "How are you?" is powerful, it's not always easy to implement. Here are some common challenges and how to overcome them:

Challenge 1: It Feels Awkward

    Solution: Practice makes perfect. Start by using the phrase with colleagues or friends until it feels natural.

Challenge 2: A Few People Give Long Responses

    Solution: If time is limited, you can respond with, "I'd love to hear more when we have time to chat properly. Thank you for sharing!"

Challenge 3: It's Not Reciprocated

    Solution: Remember that the goal is to create a positive atmosphere, not to control others' reactions. Your effort still makes a difference.

You Are Creating a Culture of Care

To truly harness the power of "How are you?" businesses and teams must embrace it as part of their culture. Here's how to make it a core value:

1. **Lead by Example:** As a leader, model the behavior you want to see. Greet everyone you encounter with "How are you?"
2. **Provide Training:** Help your team understand why this approach matters and how to implement it effectively.
3. **Celebrate Success:** Recognize and reward team members who go above and beyond in creating personal connections.
4. **Gather Feedback:** Regularly ask customers and team members how the culture of care is impacting their experience.

Practicing "How Are You?" in Daily Life

Incorporating this habit into your daily interactions can have a profound impact, not just professionally but also personally. Here's how to practice:

- **At Home:** Start your day by asking your family members "How are you?" and really listening to their answers.
- **In Your Community:** Greet neighbors, baristas, or anyone you encounter with "How are you?"
- **With Yourself:** Take a moment each day to ask yourself, "How am I?" and reflect on your well-being.

Imagine a world where everyone felt seen, valued, and cared for. It starts with a simple question: "How are you?" Whether you're a business owner, team leader, or someone who interacts with others every day, this small change can make a big difference.

So, the next time you greet someone, pause before saying, "How can I help you?" Instead, ask, "How are you?" and see the transformation unfold.

The Power of Small Talk—Building Bridges One Conversation at a Time

In the fast-paced world of customer service, small talk often gets overlooked. Yet, it holds immense potential to transform interactions from transactional to meaningful. Small talk is more than idle chatter—it's a way to build connections, show genuine interest, and leave a lasting impression.

What Is Small Talk?

Small talk is casual, polite conversation about noncontroversial topics, such as the weather, local events, or shared experiences. While it might seem insignificant, small talk creates a bridge between people, setting the stage for more meaningful engagement. In service, it can break the ice, establish rapport, and make customers feel valued.

The significance of small talk, like asking a simple "How are you?" cannot be overstated, especially when it comes to customer service. These brief interactions, while seemingly insignificant, play a key role in shaping a customer's emotional experience and perception of the service they receive. According to Pezdek and Eddy (2001), these small, affective exchanges have a lasting impact on how customers remember and feel about their service encounters.

Why Small Talk Matters

1. **It Humanizes the Interaction**

   Small talk reminds your customers that you see them as individuals, not just transactions. A quick conversation about their day, a compliment on their choice, or a comment on the weather personalize the experience.

2. **It Builds Trust and Loyalty**

   When customers feel comfortable talking to you, they're more likely to trust your recommendations and return for future interactions.

3. **It Creates Memorable Experiences**

   Customers remember how you made them feel. Small talk can make their visit enjoyable and unique, setting you apart from competitors.

4. **It Reduces Tension in Difficult Situations**

   Small talk can diffuse frustration or anxiety. A lighthearted comment can redirect the focus and put customers at ease.

Mastering the Art of Small Talk

Like any skill, small talk can be learned and perfected. Here's how:

1. **Start with Simple Observations**

   Observations are a great way to initiate small talk. For example:
   - "It's such a beautiful day today!"
   - "I see you picked the chocolate cake—that's one of my favorites too!"

2. **Use Open-Ended Questions**

   Questions that can't be answered with a simple "yes" or "no" encourage conversation. Examples include:
   - "What brings you in today?"
   - "Have you tried our new menu item yet?"

3. **Listen Actively**

   Pay attention to the customer's responses and build on them. If they mention they're celebrating a birthday, respond with enthusiasm and follow-up:
   - "Happy birthday! How are you celebrating?"

4. **Keep It Positive and Light**

   Avoid controversial or overly personal topics. Stick to friendly, neutral subjects that create a pleasant atmosphere.

5. **Be Genuine**

   Authenticity is key. Customers can sense when small talk is forced or insincere. Show genuine interest in what they say.

Small Talk in Action

Let's look at examples of small talk tailored to different service scenarios:

Scenario 1: A Coffee Shop

Customer: *"I'll have a latte, please."*

You: *"Coming right up! Busy day ahead or taking it easy?"*

Scenario 2: A Retail Store

Customer: *"Do you have this in a smaller size?"*

You: *"Let me check for you. That's a great choice—this style has been really popular!"*

Scenario 3: A Hotel Reception

Customer: *"I'm here to check in."*

You: *"Welcome! Is this your first time visiting the city?"*

The Benefits of Small Talk for Your Business

1. **It Encourages Repeat Visits**

   When customers feel valued, they're more likely to return. A friendly conversation can be the difference between a one-time customer and a loyal regular.

2. **It Increases Sales**

   Small talk builds trust, making customers more open to your suggestions. For example:
   - "If you liked this, you might also enjoy our new product."

3. **It Boosts Employee Morale**

   Encouraging small talk among team members and customers creates a positive work environment. Employees feel more connected to their roles and the people they serve.

Overcoming Challenges in Small Talk

Not everyone is naturally comfortable with small talk. Here's how to navigate common challenges:

1. **Shyness or Introversion**
   If you're introverted, start small. Practice with simple comments like, *"How's your day going?"* Over time, you'll feel more confident.

2. **Unresponsive Customers**
   Not all customers will engage in small talk, and that's okay. Respect their preference and focus on providing excellent service. You will eventually be able to see each customer differently and know if they want small talk or not. It becomes your sense.

3. **Balancing Efficiency and Connection**
   In busy environments, time is limited. Even a brief comment—like *"I hope you enjoy this!"*—can make an impact without slowing you down.

Stories of Success Through Small Talk

Case Study 1: The Restaurant with a Personal Touch

A restaurant transformed its service by training the team to engage in small talk. The team would ask about customers' weekends or comment on their favorite pastries. Sales increased as customers began coming back for the friendly atmosphere as much as the baked goods.

Case Study 2: The Hotel Concierge

A hotel concierge made it a point to ask every guest, *"What brings you to town?"* This simple question led to countless opportunities to offer personalized recommendations, earning rave reviews and repeat business.

Making Small Talk Part of Your Culture

For small talk to become second nature, it must be embedded in your team's culture.

1. **Lead by Example**

   Managers should model effective small talk during daily interactions.

2. **Provide Training**

   Role-playing exercises can help team members practice initiating and sustaining small talk.

3. **Celebrate Successes**

   Recognize employees who excel at using small talk to enhance customer experiences.

Small Talk as a Superpower

Small talk may seem small, but its impact is immense. It's the foundation of connection, the secret to loyalty, and a powerful tool for creating unforgettable experiences.

When you take the time to engage in small talk, you're not just filling the silence—you're building a bridge, one conversation at a time.

As you apply this principle, remember that every interaction is an opportunity to brighten someone's day, one friendly word at a time.

"Say My Name—The Personal Touch That Builds Loyalty"

There's something magical about hearing your name. It's one of the first words we learn to recognize, and it carries a deep sense of identity. In customer service, using a customer's name is a powerful tool that can transform an interaction from ordinary to exceptional. It signals that the customer is more than just a transaction—they are a valued individual.

Why Names Matter in Service

1. **It's Personal**

   Using someone's name makes the interaction feel personal. It shows that you see them as an individual, not just another customer in a queue. This small gesture can make a significant impact, leaving them with a positive memory of your service.

2. **It Builds Trust**

   When you use a customer's name, it creates a sense of familiarity and trust. People are naturally more comfortable when they feel recognized. Trust is the cornerstone of customer loyalty, and using a name is an easy way to foster it.

3. **It Grabs Attention**

   A name is like a magnet for attention. When someone hears their name, they instinctively focus on the speaker. This makes it a great tool for engaging customers and ensuring they feel connected to the interaction.

4. **It Encourages Repeat Business**

   Customers who feel valued are more likely to return. Using their name shows that you remember them, and this sense of acknowledgment can create a deeper bond with your business.

The Science Behind Names

Studies in neuroscience have shown that hearing one's own name activates different areas of the brain, including those associated with self-identity and emotional processing. This explains why people respond so positively when their name is used—it's tied to their sense of self.

In service, this science translates to increased customer satisfaction and a stronger emotional connection with your brand.

How to Incorporate Names into Service

1. **Learn It Quickly**

   Make it a priority to learn and use a customer's name early in the interaction. If they make a reservation, check in, or place an order, use the information they provide to address them by name.

   - Example: *"Welcome, Sarah! Thank you for choosing us today."*

2. **Use It Naturally**

   While it's important to use a customer's name, it should never feel forced. Use it naturally within the flow of conversation, and avoid overusing it to the point where it feels insincere.

   - Example: *"John, your coffee is ready. Is there anything else I can get for you?"*

3. **Make It Memorable**

   If possible, make an effort to remember the names of regular customers. This creates a deeper connection and makes them feel genuinely valued.

   ○ Example: *"Good to see you again, Lisa! The usual today?"*

4. **Confirm Pronunciations**

   If you're unsure how to pronounce someone's name, don't hesitate
   to ask. People appreciate the effort, and it shows that you care
   about getting it right.

   ○ Example: *"I want to make sure I say your name correctly—how do
   you pronounce it?"*

5. **Train Your Team**

   Encourage your team to use names whenever possible. Share tips
   on how to remember names and integrate them naturally into
   conversations.

Examples of Using Names in Different Fields

Hospitality

When a guest checks into a hotel:

○ *"Welcome, Mr. Davis. We're so glad to have you with us. If you
need anything, don't hesitate to reach out."*

Retail

At the checkout counter:

○ *"Thank you for shopping with us, Emily. Have a wonderful day!"*

Cafés and Restaurants

When serving a regular:

○ *"Hi, Tom! Your usual table is ready. Let me know if there's anything special you'd like today."*

Health Care

When greeting a patient:

○ *"Good morning, Mrs. Johnson. How are you feeling today?"*

While using names is powerful, there are a few challenges to
consider:

○ **Remembering Names:** It can be difficult to remember every
name, especially in a busy environment. Using tools like a reservation system or loyalty program can help.

- ○ **Mispronunciations**: Mispronouncing a name can make someone feel unseen. If in doubt, always ask for clarification.
- ○ **Overuse**: While using a name is impactful, overusing it can come across as insincere or even salesy. Aim for balance.

Techniques for Remembering Names

1. **Repeat It**
   When someone introduces themselves, repeat their name back to them.
   - ○ Example: *"Nice to meet you, Mark!"*
2. **Associate It**
   Create an association with their name to help you remember it. For example, if a customer named Daisy loves flowers, connect her name to that fact.
3. **Write It Down**
   If appropriate, jot down names in a customer log or loyalty program. This is especially helpful for regulars.
4. **Use Mnemonics**
   Develop memory aids to help you remember names. For instance, if a customer's name is Peter and he always orders pie, you can link "Peter" to "pie."

The Impact of Using Names

1. **Customer Loyalty**
   Customers are more likely to return when they feel personally acknowledged. Using their name is a simple yet effective way to build this loyalty.
2. **Positive Reviews**
   When customers feel valued, they're more likely to leave positive reviews and recommend your business to others.
3. **Emotional Connection**
   Using a name creates an emotional connection, turning a routine interaction into a memorable experience.

Anecdotes: Real Stories of Name Impact

1. **The Regular Who Became a Promoter**

   At a local café, a customer named Samantha became a loyal regular because the team remembered her name and favorite drink. She often brought friends and shared glowing reviews online.

2. **The Nervous Guest**

   A hotel guest who was nervous about a presentation felt reassured when the front desk staff addressed him by name and wished him good luck. He later mentioned in a review how this small gesture boosted his confidence.

Conclusion: Say Their Name

In the world of customer service, personalization is everything. Using a customer's name is one of the simplest ways to create a meaningful connection, foster loyalty, and elevate their experience. It's a small effort that can lead to big rewards.

Remember, it's not just about saying the name—it's about how you say it. Use it with warmth, sincerity, and respect, and you'll transform your interactions into moments that customers will remember and cherish.

Let's start building those connections, one name at a time.

The Power of Knowing the Customer's Needs Before They Even Know Them

One of the highest levels of service is anticipating a customer's needs before they even express them. This skill sets apart an exceptional service provider from an average one. When you understand your customers well enough, you can predict their wants, preferences, and concerns before they verbalize them.

Observing Cues

Watch for nonverbal hints—body language, facial expressions, and tone of voice can reveal a lot about a customer's mood and expectations.

A hesitant glance at the menu, a slow approach to the counter, or a sigh can all signal an opportunity to step in and assist.

Learning Patterns

Regular customers often have preferences. Remembering these details and acting on them without being asked build loyalty and trust.

Example: A café employee who remembers a regular's usual order and starts preparing it as soon as they walk in creates a seamless and personalized experience. This kind of service makes customers feel seen and valued.

Proactive Solutions

Instead of waiting for a request, offer assistance ahead of time. A refill before they ask, a recommendation based on their past choices, or providing a necessary item without prompting make a customer feel truly cared for.

Example: A hotel concierge who notices a guest struggling with luggage and immediately offers a cart without being asked creates a moment of exceptional service.

Why This Matters

Customers may not always know exactly what they need, but, when you anticipate it for them, they experience a level of service that feels effortless and seamless. This leads to higher customer satisfaction, positive reviews, and increased loyalty.

Every interaction is an opportunity to create a positive experience. Your actions define the business in the eyes of every customer you serve. Be intentional, be present, and, most importantly, be the person who makes customers return—not because they have to but because they want to.

You are not just an employee—you are the business. Make every moment count.

Genuine Versus Scripted

Being yourself in service is one of the most important things you can do. Even though there are specific things we need to check off, it is crucial to put our own authentic selves into the experience. Customers can tell when someone is speaking from a script versus when they are genuinely engaged. The key to exceptional service is balancing structure with personality.

I once worked for a global company that emphasized service, and one of the requirements was that every Front-of-House (FOH) team member ask each customer if they had visited before. While well-intended, this scripted approach often felt robotic. We knew that our level of service was paramount, and we needed to ensure that customers felt welcomed and valued, not like they were just another transaction. Customers want to feel seen and appreciated, and that means engaging with them in a natural and personalized way.

To solve this, we adjusted our approach. For customers we recognized, we greeted them with "Welcome back! How are you?" rather than following a rigid script. This small change made a significant impact, as it instantly created a sense of familiarity and appreciation. Returning customers felt acknowledged, and that strengthened their connection to our brand.

For new customers, instead of repeating the same question the same way every time, we trained the team to vary their phrasing while still gathering the necessary information. Some examples included:

- "Have you dined with us before?"
- "Have you had the chance to visit our Brisbane team before?"
- "What is your favorite location?"
- "Is this your first time experiencing our menu?"

By introducing variation and personalization, we ensured that our service remained both structured and warm. The goal was never to abandon the system but rather to humanize it. The best service follows a strong foundation while allowing room for genuine, personalized connections with customers. That is the balance between systemized service and authentic hospitality.

Customers can sense when a greeting or question is forced, and it can immediately impact their perception of the service they are about to receive. A robotic approach can make customers feel like just another transaction rather than a valued guest. Instead, when a greeting is warm and personalized, it sets the tone for a positive experience.

Beyond just varying phrasing, tone of voice plays an essential role. Someone can say "Have you dined with us before?" in a monotonous, uninterested way, or they can ask the same question with enthusiasm and warmth. The difference is striking. Encouraging team members to embrace natural conversation, instead of rigid compliance, elevates the guest experience.

Additionally, nonverbal cues such as eye contact, facial expressions, and body language add another layer to genuine service. Smiling while greeting a customer, leaning in slightly when engaging in conversation, and maintaining friendly eye contact, all communicate warmth and attentiveness. When employees are fully present and engaged, customers can feel the sincerity in their interactions.

One of the most compelling aspects of genuine service is how it fosters customer loyalty. When people feel an authentic connection with a brand or business, they are more likely to return. I have witnessed firsthand how these small but meaningful changes have transformed customer relationships. Guests who might have been one-time visitors became regulars simply because of the way they were welcomed and treated.

Another key element of moving beyond scripted service is listening. When employees actively listen to customers and respond naturally rather than sticking to a rigid script, it builds trust. For example, if a customer mentions they are celebrating a birthday or an anniversary, acknowledging that moment and offering something special—whether a kind remark or a small complimentary treat—goes a long way in making the experience memorable.

This approach also benefits the employees themselves. When team members are encouraged to bring their personalities into their interactions, they enjoy their work more. Being able to engage naturally with customers creates a more fulfilling and rewarding work environment. Employees feel empowered when they are not confined to a script but rather guided by principles of great service.

Ultimately, the power of extending genuine versus scripted courtesy lies in the ability to balance consistency with authenticity. While certain standards and guidelines are necessary to maintain quality service, the real magic happens when employees feel confident enough to personalize their interactions. Customers respond to sincerity, and when they feel genuinely welcomed and valued, they will keep coming back. That is the true essence of hospitality.

The Power of Touch—The Subtle Art of Connection

Touch is one of the most powerful and immediate forms of communication. It transcends words, conveying warmth, care, and a sense of human connection. However, when we talk about "the power of touch" in customer service, we're not referring to anything that crosses personal boundaries. Rather, we're discussing the small, respectful gestures that make people feel seen, heard, and valued. A light touch on the arm, a friendly handshake, or a pat on the back can make all the difference in how someone perceives an interaction.

We will explore how touch can enhance your service delivery, create stronger bonds with customers, and convey care in a subtle yet impactful way.

What Is the Power of Touch?

Touch is a fundamental part of human connection. From an early age, we learn that touch can comfort, reassure, and communicate emotions. In service, the power of touch is about creating an emotional connection without overstepping boundaries. It's the gentle pat on the back of a colleague after a busy shift, the light touch on a customer's arm when thanking them, or the friendly handshake that closes a successful interaction.

These small gestures of touch foster trust and convey empathy. They help create an atmosphere where customers feel like more than just transactions—they feel like people whose presence is appreciated.

Why Touch Matters in Service

1. **It Humanizes the Interaction**

   In an increasingly digital world, human connection can sometimes feel lost. Touch helps bring us back to our humanity. A brief, appropriate touch can show that you care beyond simply doing your job. It can turn a standard service interaction into something memorable and personal.

2. **It Conveys Care and Respect**

   A simple touch can communicate a lot about how you feel toward a customer. For example, when you thank a customer and give them a light touch on the arm, you're subtly conveying your appreciation for their business. It shows that you are invested in their experience, not just in the transaction.

3. **It Creates Emotional Bonds**

   The power of touch lies in its ability to create emotional connections. When someone touches your arm gently while expressing thanks, or when you receive a handshake, it creates a sense of mutual respect and understanding. These connections are what keep customers returning—they remember how you made them feel, not just what you sold them.

4. **It Can Convey Confidence and Reassurance**

   A quick, confident touch can communicate a sense of calm and security. Whether it's reassuring a nervous customer or giving a colleague a pat on the back, touch can provide comfort and instill confidence, both in your customer and in yourself.

The Psychology Behind Touch

Research has shown that touch can trigger emotional responses in the brain. When you experience touch, even something as simple as a handshake or a pat on the back, your body releases oxytocin—the "feel-good" hormone. Oxytocin is linked to bonding and emotional connection, which is why touch can leave a lasting impression on a customer.

Furthermore, studies have shown that customers are more likely to return to a business where they feel treated with kindness, respect, and human connection. A simple, nonintrusive touch can be an integral part of this positive experience. Gallace and Spence (2010) explore the science behind interpersonal touch, emphasizing its profound impact on human interactions. In a service setting, touch—when appropriate and culturally sensitive—can enhance customer experiences by fostering warmth, trust, and a sense of connection. Their research suggests that even subtle forms of touch, such as a light pat on the shoulder or a handshake, can positively influence perceptions of service quality and satisfaction. This aligns with the idea that tactile interactions can create a more personalized and emotionally engaging experience, reinforcing the importance of human connection in customer service.

When to Use Touch in Service

It's important to remember that touch must always be appropriate, respectful, and consensual. Knowing when and how to use touch is essential to creating a positive experience both for you and your customer.

1. **Thanking Customers**

   A light touch on the arm or shoulder when thanking a customer can convey genuine appreciation. For example:
   - "Thank you for coming in today," accompanied by a light touch on the arm, can make the gesture feel warmer and more heartfelt.

2. **Wishing Well**

   When customers are leaving, a simple "Have a great day!" along with a small touch can show that you wish them well beyond the transaction. For example, a light touch on the upper arm or a handshake can make your wish feel more sincere.

3. **Offering Comfort**

   In difficult situations, such as when a customer is upset, a reassuring touch on the hand or shoulder (if it feels appropriate) can convey empathy and show that you genuinely care about their experience. It's important that your touch doesn't feel forced or out of place; it should feel natural and aligned with your intention to comfort.

4. **Acknowledging Achievements**

   For your team, a light touch on the back or shoulder can be a powerful way to acknowledge a job well done. It's a nonverbal way of showing that you're proud of them, fostering a positive work environment.

The Subtlety of Touch—Respecting Boundaries

While touch can be a powerful tool, it is important to understand that everyone has different comfort levels. What feels appropriate to one person might be uncomfortable for another. It's essential to always respect personal space and cultural differences when incorporating touch into your service style.

In any customer service setting, it's crucial to be mindful of:

- **Personal Boundaries:** Not everyone may be comfortable with physical touch. Always pay attention to body language and adjust your approach accordingly.
- **Cultural Sensitivity:** Different cultures have varying norms around physical touch. What is acceptable in one culture may not be in another, so it's essential to be aware of these differences when interacting with customers from diverse backgrounds.
- **Context:** The setting and the situation should always inform your decision to use touch. A friendly tap on the arm may be welcomed in a casual setting but may not be appropriate in more formal or professional environments.

Examples of Touch in Action

Example 1: Retail Setting

> **Customer:** *"This is exactly what I was looking for. Thank you!"*
> **You:** *"I'm so glad you found it! Enjoy your new purchase"* (light touch on their arm or shoulder).

Example 2: Coffee Shop

> **Customer:** *"I'll take a cappuccino, thanks!"*
> **You:** *"Coming right up!"* (handing over the drink with a friendly handshake or a light touch on the arm).

Example 3: Hotel Check-In

> **Customer:** *"I'm so excited for this vacation!"*
> **You:** *"I hope it's everything you imagined and more!"* (light touch on the shoulder or upper arm to convey warmth and good wishes).

The Benefits of Touch for Your Business

1. **Creating a Memorable Experience**

   A simple touch, when done right, can enhance the emotional experience of a customer. It can make them feel more connected to your brand and encourage them to return for future visits.

2. **Building Customer Loyalty**

   Customers want to feel valued. When they experience personalized service, complete with thoughtful gestures like touch, they're more likely to return and recommend your business to others.

3. **Enhancing Team Morale**

   Touch isn't just for customers—it can also be an important tool for team bonding. A light tap on the back after a job well done, a handshake at the start of a shift, or a friendly touch to show appreciation, all contribute to a supportive work environment.

   The power of touch in service is subtle but incredibly impactful. It conveys warmth, care, and human connection. When done respectfully and thoughtfully, touch can leave a lasting impression on customers, turning a simple service interaction into a moment of emotional connection.

   As you consider how to incorporate touch into your service, remember to always be mindful of boundaries, context, and cultural differences. When done right, touch will be a tool that helps you create stronger, more meaningful relationships with both your customers and your team.

CHAPTER 3

The Silent Language of Service: Eye Contact and Body Language

The Power of the Eyes

Eye contact is one of the most powerful nonverbal tools we possess. In the delivery of exceptional service, it can communicate trust, attentiveness, and empathy—qualities that are foundational to building connections and exceeding customer expectations. Despite its simplicity, eye contact is often overlooked or underutilized in service settings. This section of the book delves into the significance of eye contact, how it can transform interactions, and practical ways to master it as a service professional.

Why Eye Contact Matters

Eye contact is the gateway to connection. It's the first step in establishing a relationship with someone, whether it's a customer, client, or colleague. Here's why it's so essential in service delivery:

1. **Builds Trust**
   When you look someone in the eye, you demonstrate sincerity and transparency. It reassures the other person that you are engaged and trustworthy.
2. **Conveys Attention**
   Eye contact signals that the person in front of you has your undivided attention, making them feel valued and respected.
3. **Expresses Empathy**
   By maintaining eye contact, you show that you're genuinely interested in the other person's feelings, needs, or concerns.

4. **Enhances Communication**

   Eye contact strengthens verbal communication, helping to reinforce your words and clarify your intentions.

5. **Creates a Positive Impression**

   A warm, confident gaze leaves a lasting impression, setting the tone for a positive interaction.

Research shows that eye contact activates social areas of the brain, creating a sense of connection and mutual understanding. It also triggers the release of oxytocin, sometimes referred to as the "bonding hormone," which fosters trust and closeness. Thus, eye contact plays a crucial role in building trust, attentiveness, and emotional connection. Research by Montague et al. (2011) highlights how eye contact significantly impacts interpersonal interactions, particularly in service and health care settings, where it fosters empathy and strengthens relationships. Their study found that patients perceived higher levels of empathy from physicians who maintained consistent eye contact, reinforcing the idea that direct gaze enhances the quality of human connection. In a service environment, the same principle applies—eye contact assures customers that they are valued and heard, ultimately improving their experience and satisfaction. Conversely, a lack of eye contact can lead to feelings of neglect or disengagement, undermining the service relationship. By mastering the art of maintaining appropriate eye contact, service professionals can create a more welcoming, trustworthy, and customer-focused atmosphere, ensuring that each interaction leaves a lasting positive impression (Montague et al. 2011).

Eye Contact in Different Service Scenarios

Eye contact plays a pivotal role in various aspects of service delivery. Let's explore its impact in specific scenarios:

1. **Greeting Customers**

   When you welcome a customer with direct eye contact, it sets a positive tone for the interaction. It shows that you're present and ready to assist, making the customer feel acknowledged.

2. **Listening to Concerns**

   Maintaining eye contact while listening to a customer's question or complaint demonstrates that you're fully engaged. It assures them that their concerns are being taken seriously.

3. **Offering Recommendations**

   When suggesting products or services, eye contact builds trust in your expertise. It helps convey confidence and genuine interest in meeting the customer's needs.

4. **Closing the Interaction**

   Ending an interaction with a sincere "Thank you" and direct eye contact leaves a lasting positive impression, encouraging customers to return.

The Cultural Context of Eye Contact

While eye contact is generally seen as a positive and necessary part of communication, cultural norms can influence how it's perceived. For example:

- **Western Cultures:** Direct eye contact is often associated with confidence and respect.
- **Asian Cultures:** Prolonged eye contact may be considered confrontational or disrespectful.
- **Middle Eastern Cultures:** Eye contact is valued, but its intensity may vary based on gender and social dynamics.

As a service professional, it's important to be aware of these cultural nuances and adapt your approach accordingly.

Real-Life Examples of Eye Contact in Action

Case Study 1: Transforming a Transactional Experience

At a retail store, a customer approached the counter with an armful of items. The cashier, distracted by another task, barely glanced at them. The customer felt ignored and left frustrated. In contrast, another cashier greeted the same customer on a different day with a smile and steady eye contact, creating a friendly and attentive atmosphere. The customer not only completed their purchase but also expressed appreciation for the excellent service.

Case Study 2: Resolving Conflict Through Eye Contact

During a busy lunch rush at a café, a customer grew upset over a delay. The manager approached with calmness, maintained steady eye contact, and listened attentively. This simple act diffused the tension, and the customer left feeling heard and valued despite the initial inconvenience.

How to Practice Effective Eye Contact

Developing strong eye contact skills takes practice and self-awareness. Here are some tips to help you master this essential aspect of service:

1. **Start with a Smile**
   Pairing eye contact with a genuine smile immediately creates warmth and approachability.
2. **Strike a Balance**
   Avoid staring, as it can feel intimidating. Aim for natural, periodic eye contact, breaking away occasionally to avoid discomfort.
3. **Be Present**
   Focus on the person in front of you, rather than being distracted by your surroundings. This enhances the quality of your eye contact.
4. **Practice Active Listening**
   Combine eye contact with nodding or verbal affirmations to show that you're fully engaged in the conversation.
5. **Adjust for Comfort**
   If someone seems uncomfortable with prolonged eye contact, respect their boundaries by shifting your gaze occasionally.

Overcoming Challenges

Making and maintaining eye contact can feel awkward or intimidating, especially for those who are shy or inexperienced in customer service. Here's how to overcome common challenges:

Challenge 1: Nervousness

Solution: Practice with colleagues or friends in a low-pressure setting to build confidence.

Challenge 2: Distractions

Solution: Train yourself to focus solely on the customer during interactions, blocking out external distractions. I once trained a young lady who was extremely shy and suffered from anxiety, and I explained to her that when she applied for a role within a service industry, eye contact was the part she struggled with. We started with imaging glue sticking her eyes together with the customers as she pulled away, the glue kept pulling them together. This was a mental cue to remind her to keep looking at the customer when she felt compelled to look away. In weeks she nailed it, and the role helped her develop her skills.

Challenge 3: Cultural Sensitivity

Solution: Learn about the cultural norms of your customer base and adjust your approach to suit their preferences.

When service professionals consistently practice effective eye contact, the benefits extend beyond individual interactions:

- **For Customers:** They feel valued, respected, and connected to the business.
- **For Teams:** Eye contact fosters stronger communication and collaboration among team members.
- **For Businesses:** Positive customer experiences lead to loyalty, referrals, and increased revenue.

Incorporating Eye Contact into Team Training

To ensure that your team excels in making eye contact, consider the following training strategies:

1. **Role-Playing Scenarios:** Practice common service interactions where eye contact plays a key role.
2. **Feedback Sessions:** Provide constructive feedback on team members' use of eye contact during real or simulated interactions.

3. **Visual Reminders:** Display posters or guidelines that emphasize the importance of eye contact.
4. **Celebrate Success:** Recognize and reward team members who excel in creating meaningful connections through eye contact.

Strong eye contact doesn't just improve professional interactions—it also enhances personal relationships and self-confidence. Practicing this skill in daily life can lead to deeper connections with friends, family, and colleagues.

Eye contact is more than a service technique—it's a powerful tool for human connection. As you interact with customers, colleagues, and others in your life, make a conscious effort to use eye contact to its full potential.

The next time you greet someone, listen to their concerns, or offer assistance, look them in the eye while you do so. Show them that they have your attention, your respect, and your care. You'll not only transform their experience but also transform yourself as a service professional.

The Power of Body Language—What Is Your Body Saying?

Words are only part of the story of human interaction. In fact, research shows that much of communication is nonverbal, conveyed through our posture, gestures, facial expressions, and movements. Body language can strengthen relationships, convey confidence, and even diffuse conflict. For service professionals, understanding and mastering body language are an essential skill—it directly impacts how customers perceive your intentions and how they feel about the interaction.

Let's explore the incredible power of body language, what it communicates, and how to use it to elevate your service.

Why Body Language Matters in Service

Body language is a silent communicator that speaks volumes. Here's why it's so important in a service setting:

1. **Reinforces Verbal Communication**
   Your words gain credibility when your body language aligns with them. For example, saying "I'd love to help" while leaning forward and smiling conveys sincerity.

2. **Builds Trust and Rapport**

   Open and approachable body language invites connection and builds trust, encouraging customers to engage with you.

3. **Displays Confidence**

   Confident posture and gestures reassure customers that you are competent and capable.

4. **Reveals Intentions**

   Even when you're not speaking, your body language reveals your attitude, mood, and level of engagement.

5. **Diffuses Tension**

   Calm and composed body language can help de-escalate conflicts and create a more positive environment.

What Your Body Might Be Saying Without Words

Let's examine common forms of body language and their potential interpretations in a service context:

Posture

- **Open Posture:** Standing tall, with your shoulders relaxed and arms uncrossed, conveys confidence and approachability.
- **Closed Posture:** Crossing your arms or slouching may suggest disinterest, defensiveness, or lack of energy.

Gestures

- **Positive Gestures:** Nodding, open hand movements, and mirroring the customer's gestures signal attentiveness and agreement.
- **Negative Gestures:** Fidgeting, pointing, or excessive movements can convey nervousness or aggression.

Facial Expressions

- **Smiling:** A genuine smile communicates warmth and positivity, making customers feel welcome.
- **Neutral or Negative Expressions:** A blank or frowning expression can create distance and discomfort.

Eye Contact

- Direct eye contact conveys engagement, while avoiding eye contact can signal disinterest, dishonesty, or discomfort.

Proximity

- **Appropriate Distance:** Respecting personal space shows consideration and professionalism.
- **Too Close or Too Far:** Standing too close may feel intrusive while standing too far may seem disengaged.

The Impact of Body Language on Customer Experience

In service delivery, body language can be the difference between a satisfied customer and a dissatisfied one. Consider these scenarios:

Scenario 1: A Warm Welcome

A customer walks into a café, and the staff member greets them with a smile, maintains eye contact, and has an open, welcoming posture. The customer feels valued and at ease, setting the tone for a positive experience.

Scenario 2: A Missed Opportunity

The same customer visits another day and is greeted by a staff member who avoids eye contact, slouches behind the counter, and appears distracted. The customer feels unimportant and may be less likely to return.

Common Body Language Mistakes in Service

1. **Lack of Awareness**
   Service professionals may not realize how their body language comes across. For example, checking a phone or crossing arms can unintentionally signal disinterest.
2. **Over-Energy or Under-Energy**
   Excessive movement or overly rigid posture can be off-putting. Striking a balance between energy and calmness is key.

3. **Ignoring Cultural Differences**

   In some cultures, specific gestures or postures may have different meanings. Being culturally sensitive is crucial in diverse environments.

How to Use Body Language Effectively in Service

1. **Start with Self-Awareness**

   Pay attention to your body language throughout the day. Consider asking a colleague for feedback or practicing in front of a mirror.

2. **Align Your Body with Your Words**

   When you say, "I'm happy to help," make sure your posture, gestures, and facial expressions reflect enthusiasm and willingness.

3. **Adopt Open and Approachable Postures**

   Stand tall, relax your shoulders, and keep your arms uncrossed. These simple adjustments make you appear more confident and friendly.

4. **Use Gestures to Reinforce Your Message**

   For example, when pointing out an item on a menu, use a smooth and deliberate gesture rather than abrupt or dismissive movements.

5. **Mirror the Customer's Body Language**

   Subtly mimicking a customer's gestures or posture can create a sense of connection and rapport.

6. **Practice Active Listening with Your Body**

   Show that you're listening by nodding, leaning slightly forward, and maintaining eye contact.

Practical Exercises to Improve Body Language

Exercise 1: Record and Review

Record yourself during a service interaction and watch the playback to identify areas for improvement.

Exercise 2: Role-Playing

Practice interactions with a colleague, focusing on maintaining positive body language throughout.

Exercise 3: Daily Check-In

Take a moment each day to evaluate your posture, facial expressions, and gestures. Adjust as needed to align with a positive and professional image.

Stories of Transformation Through Body Language

Case Study 1: The Restaurant Turnaround

At a struggling restaurant, staff were trained to adopt open, confident postures and to greet customers warmly. The change in body language alone created a friendlier atmosphere, leading to increased customer satisfaction and repeat business.

Case Study 2: The Sales Boost

A retail team learned to use body language intentionally, such as smiling, nodding, and mirroring customers. Sales increased as customers felt more comfortable and engaged during their shopping experience.

Adapting to Virtual and Digital Interactions

With the rise of virtual meetings and digital service channels, body language is still relevant—albeit in different ways. Here's how to adapt:

1. **In Video Calls:** Maintain good posture, look at the camera to simulate eye contact, and use expressive gestures to engage viewers.
2. **In Text-Based Communication:** Your "body language" comes through in your tone and word choice. Use friendly, professional language to convey warmth and attentiveness.

Body Language as a Team Culture

When an entire team adopts positive body language, it creates a consistent and welcoming environment. Leaders can foster this culture by:

- Providing regular training on nonverbal communication
- Leading by example with their own body language
- Encouraging team members to support and coach one another

Your body speaks before you say a word. It has the power to shape perceptions, build relationships, and transform customer experiences. By mastering your body language, you can elevate your service to extraordinary levels.

The next time you interact with a customer, ask yourself: *"What is my body saying right now?"* With practice, you can ensure that your body language always communicates professionalism, warmth, and genuine care.

Exceeding Expectations Before They Walk Through the Door

Every customer who walks through the door already has expectations. Whether they are stepping into a café for their morning coffee, checking into a hotel, or walking into a retail store, they carry with them an idea of what their experience should be like. These expectations are shaped by past experiences, reviews, brand reputation, and personal desires. As service professionals, our job isn't just to meet these expectations—it's to exceed them in ways that leave a lasting impression.

The Power of First Impressions

Long before a customer interacts with you directly, their expectations are being formed. A business's website, social media presence, and even word-of-mouth, all play a role in shaping what a customer anticipates. But the real magic happens in the first few moments of an in-person experience.

From the moment they enter the business, customers observe and absorb everything—the cleanliness, the ambience, the attentiveness of the team, and the overall energy of the space. If you are intentional about ensuring that the first impression is warm, welcoming, and professional, you set the tone for a superior experience.

Key Strategies for Exceeding First Impressions

- Ensure the environment is inviting—clean, well-lit, and aesthetically pleasing.
- The team should be visible, approachable, and ready to engage.

- Immediate acknowledgment—even a simple smile or eye contact—can make a world of difference.
- A proactive greeting that goes beyond the generic "How can I help you?" Instead, personalize it: "Welcome in! How are you today?"

Customers may not always articulate their needs, but they still expect certain things to happen seamlessly. A great service professional learns to anticipate these needs before the customer even realizes them.

For example:

- A regular guest at a restaurant may not need to ask for extra napkins if a server notices they frequently request them.
- A barista may see a customer shivering and proactively offer a warm beverage suggestion.
- A hotel receptionist may notice a weary traveler and instinctively expedite the check-in process.

These small yet impactful gestures create an effortless experience where customers feel cared for without needing to ask for what they need.

The Extra 10 Percent

Meeting expectations is standard. Delivering 10 percent more than expected is what sets businesses apart. It's about adding value in ways that make customers feel valued.

Ways to deliver the extra 10 percent:

- Personalization: Use a customer's name and remember small details about their preferences.
- Anticipation: If you know that a particular product or service is popular, have it ready before customers ask.
- Exceeding Speed Expectations: If a service is expected to take 10 minutes, aim to complete it in 8.
- Surprise and Delight: Offer a complimentary item, an upgrade, or simply a handwritten thank-you note.

Managing Expectations to Avoid Disappointment

While exceeding expectations is the goal, it is also crucial to manage them appropriately. Overpromising and underdelivering is one of the fastest ways to break trust. Instead, be transparent about what can be done and then find ways to deliver above that mark.

For example:

- If a product will take 5 to 7 business days to arrive, communicate the full timeframe but aim to get it to the customer in 4.
- If a table at a restaurant will be ready in 20 minutes, check in with the guest at the 15-minute mark with an update or a small token of appreciation for their patience.

When customers walk away with an experience that goes beyond what they anticipated, they don't just return—they become brand ambassadors. They tell their friends, leave glowing reviews, and develop loyalty that competitors will struggle to break.

Businesses that prioritize service excellence recognize that every interaction is an opportunity to create this kind of loyalty.

Exceeding customer expectations is not a one-time effort—it's a mindset. It requires observation, anticipation, and a genuine commitment to making each customer feel valued. When service professionals embrace this, they transform routine transactions into memorable experiences. And that is what sets truly exceptional businesses apart from the rest.

Earning the Right to Be Casual:
The Art of Professional Warmth

In the world of exceptional service, the way we address and interact with customers sets the foundation for trust and respect. Too often, businesses assume that a casual, friendly tone from the outset will make customers feel welcome. However, the truth is that informality is not a given; it is something that must be earned. Understanding when and how to transition from formality to familiarity is an essential skill that separates good service from world-class service.

The Power of Professionalism

When a customer walks through the door, they bring with them a set of expectations. These expectations include being treated with courtesy, respect, and attentiveness. Greeting a new customer with a casual "Hey mate" or "What's up, buddy?" may feel friendly, but it can come across as overly familiar, dismissive, or even unprofessional. Instead, starting with a more formal approach—such as "Good morning, sir," "Welcome, ma'am," or "How may I assist you today?"—demonstrates professionalism and attentiveness.

Formality does not mean stiffness or robotic service; rather, it signals that the customer is valued and respected. It provides an immediate sense of structure and assurance that they are in good hands. Customers want to feel that the business takes their presence seriously and that they will receive quality service.

Reading the Customer: Knowing When to Shift

One of the key skills in service excellence is the ability to read the room and adjust your approach accordingly. Some customers appreciate a formal tone throughout their entire interaction, while others may warm up quickly and invite a more relaxed exchange.
Pay attention to verbal and nonverbal cues:

- If a customer responds in a warm, relaxed manner and uses casual language, it may be appropriate to gradually mirror their tone.
- Regular customers who have built a rapport with you may expect a friendly and informal greeting, but it should never be assumed.
- Some customers prefer professionalism at all times, and that should always be respected.

The key is to let the customer set the tone. If they address you casually first, it's usually safe to reciprocate. If they remain formal, then mirroring that formality ensures they feel comfortable and respected.

The Role of Personalization in Building Rapport

A major part of earning the right to be casual is personalization. Addressing a customer by their name is one of the most powerful ways to create a connection while maintaining respect. Saying, "Good morning, Mr. Johnson," rather than "Hey, buddy," conveys professionalism while also adding a personal touch.

When a customer frequents a business, employees often feel inclined to shift toward familiarity. However, it is always best to allow the customer to set this standard. Some customers enjoy being greeted with a warm "Welcome back, James!" while others may prefer the more professional "Great to see you again, Mr. Smith." Knowing the difference is what makes service stand out.

The Danger of Assumed Familiarity

Assumed familiarity can be damaging in service interactions. When a business becomes too informal too quickly, it can create discomfort and even alienate customers. Overly casual greetings can:

- Undermine professionalism.
- Make certain customers feel disregarded or not taken seriously.
- Blur the boundaries of appropriate service interactions.

For example, addressing an older customer as "buddy" or "mate" may feel inappropriate, whereas maintaining a respectful distance with "sir" or "ma'am" ensures they feel valued. Likewise, using nicknames or playful remarks too soon can seem presumptive and even intrusive.

Striking the Perfect Balance

The best service providers master the balance between professionalism and warmth. They understand that formality provides a foundation of respect, while familiarity, when earned, strengthens the customer relationship. The transition should always be customer-led rather than service-led.

A successful approach looks like this:

1. **Start Formal**—Greet with professionalism: "Good afternoon, Mr. Taylor. How may I assist you today?"
2. **Observe and Adjust**—If Mr. Taylor responds casually and warmly, the next interaction may shift to "Great to see you again, John!"

3. **Maintain Respect**—Even when rapport is built, ensure that warmth never crosses into overfamiliarity that could diminish the quality of service.

True hospitality is about creating a space where customers feel comfortable, valued, and respected. While warmth and friendliness are key to great service, they must be introduced at the right moment and in the right way. Informality should never be the starting point—it is a privilege granted by the customer; it is not an automatic right. By understanding when and how to shift from formal to familiar, businesses can create meaningful connections while maintaining the highest standards of professionalism.

CHAPTER 4

Service Is a Verb: Attentiveness, Energy, and Engagement

Service Is a Verb—The Action That Drives Excellence

Service is not a passive concept. It's an action, a deliberate choice to engage, assist, and elevate the experience of others. To truly understand service, we must view it as a verb—something we actively do, with intention and purpose.

When we think of service as a verb, we see it as a series of actions that demonstrate care, attention, and value. It's about doing—not just being. This mindset pushes us to:

1. **Engage Actively**: Anticipate needs and respond proactively.
2. **Solve Problems**: Take ownership of challenges and find solutions.
3. **Build Relationships**: Actively connect with customers to create meaningful interactions.

The Mindset of Service

Seeing service as a verb requires a shift in mindset. It's no longer about checking boxes or fulfilling minimum expectations—it's about going above and beyond. Here's what this mindset entails:

1. **Empathy**: Put yourself in the customer's shoes. What would make them feel cared for?
2. **Initiative**: Don't wait for a request. Look for opportunities to serve.
3. **Consistency**: Commit to delivering the same high standard of service every time.

Service in Action: Examples from the Field

1. **Anticipating Needs**

   Imagine a diner at a restaurant whose water glass is nearly empty. Instead of waiting for them to ask for a refill, the server refills it before they notice.

   - **Action**: Look for cues that indicate what the customer might need next.
   - **Impact**: Anticipation makes the customer feel cared for and valued.

2. **Problem-Solving with Grace**

   A customer receives the wrong order at a café. Instead of defensiveness, the server apologizes sincerely, corrects the mistake, and offers a complimentary item.

   - **Action**: Own the mistake and resolve it with a positive attitude.
   - **Impact**: Turning a negative moment into a positive one builds trust and loyalty.

3. **Personalizing the Experience**

   A barista remembers a regular customer's usual order and greets them warmly.

   - **Action**: Pay attention to preferences and habits.
   - **Impact**: Personalized service creates a sense of belonging and strengthens relationships.

   These are all moments when you need to do something—serve.

Service Across Industries

1. **Hospitality**
   - **Verb**: Welcome guests, ensure comfort, resolve issues promptly, and create experience.
   - **Example**: A hotel concierge arranges a last-minute tour for a guest, ensuring their trip exceeds expectations.

2. **Retail**
   - **Verb**: Greet, assist, recommend, and ensure satisfaction.
   - **Example**: A store associate helps a customer find the perfect gift by asking thoughtful questions and offering personalized suggestions.

3. **Health Care**
   - ○ **Verb**: Care, reassure, and provide clear communication.
   - ○ **Example**: A nurse takes the time to explain a procedure, ensuring the patient feels informed and comforted.
4. **Customer Support**
   - ○ **Verb**: Listen, empathize, and resolve.
   - ○ **Example**: A support agent helps a frustrated customer troubleshoot an issue, staying calm and empathetic throughout.

Why Action Matters

When service becomes a verb, it transforms from a passive offering into an active process of creating value. Here's why that matters:

1. **It Demonstrates Commitment**
   Actions speak louder than words. Customers notice when you actively work to meet their needs.
2. **It Builds Trust**
   Consistently taking action shows reliability and builds trust over time.
3. **It Drives Results**
   Active service leads to happier customers, better reviews, and increased loyalty.

How to Embrace Service as a Verb

1. **Practice Active Listening**
   Listen not just to what the customer says but, instead, to what they need. Pay attention to tone, body language, and context.
   - ○ **Example:** A customer says, *"I'm just browsing,"* but their glance at a specific item suggests interest. Offer gentle guidance.
2. **Act Quickly**
   Respond promptly to requests and concerns. Speed shows attentiveness.
   - ○ **Example:** When a customer e-mails with a question, respond within the hour if possible.

3. **Go the Extra Mile**

   Look for ways to exceed expectations.
   - **Example:** Include a handwritten thank-you note with an online order.

4. **Collaborate**

   Service isn't a solo act. Work with your team to ensure seamless customer experiences.
   - **Example:** A server communicates with the kitchen to ensure a diner's dietary restrictions are met.

Overcoming Challenges in Active Service

1. **Time Constraints**

   In busy environments, it can be challenging to give every customer the same level of attention.

   Solution: Focus on small, meaningful actions that make a difference, like a genuine smile or a quick acknowledgment.

2. **Burnout**

   Constantly giving your best can be exhausting.

   Solution: Prioritize self-care and teamwork to share the workload.

3. **Difficult Customers**

   Not every customer will appreciate your efforts.

   Solution: Stay professional, focus on what you can control, and remember that your actions reflect your standards, not theirs.

   In my years of training FOH operations, our motto for difficult customers was, always, to kill them with kindness. If you keep reflecting positivity and kindness, you will eventually see that returned.

Measuring the Impact of Active Service

1. **Customer Feedback**

   Monitor reviews and surveys for positive mentions of actions taken by your team.

2. **Repeat Business**

   Track customer return rates to see how active service builds loyalty.

3. **Employee Satisfaction**
   Team members who see the positive impact of their actions are often more motivated and engaged.

Service in Motion

Service isn't just something we offer—it's something we do. When we embrace it as a verb, we create experiences that customers remember and value. Every interaction becomes an opportunity to act with purpose, care, and intention.

By making service an active part of your business, you'll not only meet customer expectations but also exceed them, building a reputation for excellence that sets you apart. So, let's get moving—because service is a verb, and action changes everything.

The Impact of Tone and Speech in Service

It's not just about what you say but how you say it. Your tone, pace, and choice of words can completely transform an interaction, turning a routine exchange into a memorable experience. Whether you're greeting a customer, handling a complaint, or providing assistance, the way you communicate influences how your words are received.

A friendly tone can turn a simple greeting into a warm welcome. A rushed, impersonal delivery can make even the most helpful response feel dismissive. When service professionals master the art of tone, speech pace, and language, they create interactions that feel engaging, personal, and professional.

The Power of Tone

Your tone is the emotional filter of your words. It conveys attitude, intention, and energy, sometimes more powerfully than the words themselves. Consider these different tones and their effects on customer perception:

1. **Warm and Friendly**
   Best for: Greeting customers, casual interactions, and building rapport.

Example: "Good morning! How are you today?" (said with a smile) versus "Next!" (said flatly).

A welcoming tone invites engagement and makes customers feel valued.

2. **Calm and Reassuring**

   Best for: Handling complaints, calming frustrated customers, or addressing concerns.

   Example: "I completely understand how frustrating that must be. Let me fix this for you."

   Keeping a steady, measured tone de-escalates tension and reassures customers that you're in control.

3. **Confident and Clear**

   Best for: Providing instructions, explaining policies, and handling requests.

   Example: "I can absolutely assist you with that. Here's what we'll do…."

   Confidence in your tone builds trust and signals that you know what you're doing.

The Role of Speech Pace

The speed at which you speak affects clarity, engagement, and emotional impact. The wrong pace can make customers feel rushed, bored, or even confused.

1. **Slow and Deliberate**

   Best for: Explaining complex topics, helping customers who may be unfamiliar with a process.

   Example: A hotel receptionist explaining check-in procedures: "Check-in time's at 3. You'll need your ID, and breakfast is at seven."

   "Check-in begins at 3 p.m. If you have your ID ready, I'll take care of everything for you. Breakfast is served in the lounge from 7 to 10 a.m."

   Speaking slowly and clearly enhances comprehension and makes customers feel respected.

2. **Energetic and Engaged**

   Best for: Sales, upselling, and creating excitement about a product or service.

   Example: A barista recommending a seasonal drink:

   "Yeah, we have pumpkin spice lattes."

   "Oh, our pumpkin spice latte is back! It's one of our most popular drinks—would you like to try it with whipped cream?"

   An enthusiastic pace conveys excitement, making interactions more dynamic.

3. **Balanced and Natural**

   Best for: Everyday interactions where you want to sound professional yet personable.

   Example: Answering a customer's question in a store:

   "That's a great question! Let me show you where it is."

   A balanced pace ensures you sound engaged without overwhelming the customer.

Choosing the Right Words

Words matter. The way we phrase our responses can change how a customer feels about an interaction—even in difficult situations.

1. **Use Positive Language**

   Best for: Framing situations constructively, even when delivering bad news.

   Example:

   Incorrect: "We don't have that item in stock."

   Correct: "That item is really popular! We're expecting more next week—would you like me to set one aside for you?"

   Reframing a negative statement keeps the conversation solution-focused.

2. **Personalized Phrasing**

   Best for: Creating stronger connections and showing attentiveness.

   Example:

   Incorrect: "Here's your coffee."

   Correct: "Here's your caramel latte, Sarah—enjoy!"

Using a customer's name makes the interaction feel personal and valued.

3. **Express Gratitude and Encouragement**

   Best for: Ending interactions on a positive note.

   Example:

   "Thank you for your patience!" (instead of just "Sorry for the wait").

   "I appreciate your time today!"

   Gratitude reinforces goodwill and leaves a lasting positive impression.

How Tone, Pace, and Language Work Together

Consider these two customer service examples—one ineffective, one excellent:

Example 1: Rushed and Unfriendly Interaction

Customer: "Hi, I ordered a cappuccino, but this is a latte."

Server (flat tone, rushed pace): "Oh…well, that's what the system says. You can reorder if you want."

Outcome: The customer feels dismissed and frustrated.

Example 2: Thoughtful, Engaging Interaction

Customer: "Hi, I ordered a cappuccino, but this is a latte."

Server (calm tone, friendly pace): "Oh no! I appreciate you letting me know. Let me fix that for you right away."

Outcome: The customer feels heard, valued, and satisfied.

By mastering the art of tone, pace, and language, service professionals can enhance every customer interaction, ensuring that the message not only gets across but also leaves a lasting positive impression.

Speak with warmth, confidence, and clarity.

Adjust your pace to match the situation.

Choose words that build trust and connection.

Great service isn't just about what you do—it's about how you make people feel. And that starts with the way you speak.

Service Is an Experience

Service is not just a series of transactions; it is a journey, an experience that shapes how people feel about a business. True service happens when we stop seeing interactions as simple exchanges of goods or services and start recognizing the human connections behind them. Every small detail—from a warm greeting and personalized service to empathy and gratitude—contributes to a holistic experience that makes customers feel valued and appreciated. It is through this level of attention to detail and care that we elevate the ordinary to the extraordinary.

When businesses focus solely on efficiency and numbers, they lose the essence of service. Customers are not just statistics; they are individuals with emotions, expectations, and desires. The businesses that succeed in delivering exceptional service are those that go beyond fulfilling a need—they create moments of delight, comfort, and connection. These moments are woven into the fabric of the customer's experience, transforming an interaction into a relationship.

Consider how a simple coffee order can turn into an experience. A customer walks in, and instead of just taking their order, the barista greets them by name, remembers their usual choice, and asks how their day is going and how they are. That moment of personal connection transforms what could have been a mere transaction into an experience that builds loyalty and trust. The customer feels seen and heard, and they leave not just with a coffee, but also with a feeling of being valued—something that will bring them back again and again.

This is why service must be intentional. It is the cumulative effect of eye contact, positive language, empathy, gratitude, and deep listening that creates a seamless and memorable experience. Service is not just about moving customers through a series of steps; it is about providing them with an emotional experience that connects them to the business on a deeper level. When employees approach their work with the mindset that they are creating experiences rather than processing transactions, they elevate the entire service culture. Every word, every gesture, and every action contributes to this shared experience.

Customers do not just return for products; they return for the way they feel when they interact with a business. It's the sense of belonging, the feeling that their time and presence are valued. A person might be able to get the same product or service elsewhere, but it is the exceptional experience that keeps them coming back, creating a lasting bond between the customer and the business. It is no longer about simply meeting expectations—it's about exceeding them, in ways that surprise and delight the customer.

By shifting the focus from transactions to experiences, businesses foster deeper relationships with their customers, enhance brand loyalty, and ultimately drive success. True service is an art—an experience crafted through thoughtful engagement, genuine care, and a commitment to making every interaction meaningful. Every employee in a business plays a role in crafting that experience, whether it's the barista, the manager, or the person cleaning the floors. The way everyone interacts with the customer, directly or indirectly, contributes to the customer's perception of the brand and their overall satisfaction.

Service is not just about fulfilling a transaction—it is about creating a meaningful and memorable experience. Every interaction, every smile, and every moment of engagement contribute to something much larger than a simple exchange of goods or services. When we approach service with the mindset that we are creating an experience, we shift from a trans-actional perspective to one that is truly customer-centric. This shift in perspective transforms the nature of every interaction and elevates the experience for both the customer and the employee.

Until we stop seeing transactions and start seeing the people behind them, true service will never reach its full potential. The best businesses are those that understand this fundamental truth—that service is not just about providing a product or service but also about creating an environment where customers feel seen, heard, and cared for. These businesses have a lasting impact, not just because of the products they offer but because of the relationships they build with their customers. True service is not just about meeting needs—it is about creating experiences that linger long after the transaction has ended.

The research supports this approach. Service is far more than a series of functional transactions—it is an emotional journey that defines how customers feel about a business long after the exchange is over. When service professionals shift their mindset from simply delivering products to crafting meaningful experiences, they build stronger, lasting connections with customers. As highlighted in the *Harvard Business Review* article "The New Science of Customer Emotions," businesses that succeed in creating emotional connections with their customers experience greater customer loyalty and significantly improved outcomes (Magids et al. 2015). This research reinforces the idea that every personal touch—from remembering a customer's name to expressing genuine care—can transform a routine interaction into a memorable and valued experience. By intentionally fostering emotional engagement, businesses move beyond meeting needs to creating deep, lasting relationships that drive long-term success.

Power to Read a Room

Service is more than just individual interactions; it is about understanding the environment and responding to the unspoken cues within a space. The ability to "read a room" is an essential skill that transforms service from a simple transaction into a dynamic and responsive experience.

The Unspoken Language of a Room

Every space, whether it be a café, a fine-dining restaurant, a retail store, or a corporate lobby, has an energy. That energy is created by the people within it—customers, employees, and even the physical space itself. When you walk into a room, pause for a moment and observe. What do you see? What do you feel? The ability to read a room allows you to anticipate needs, diffuse tension, and elevate the customer experience effortlessly.

Key Elements of Reading a Room

1. **Body Language**
   - Observe how people are standing or sitting. Are they relaxed or tense?
   - Look for crossed arms, fidgeting, or shifting weight—these can indicate discomfort or impatience.
   - Notice if a guest is leaning in or away from their conversation partner—this can show engagement or disinterest.
2. **Eye Contact**
   - Customers making strong eye contact with you may need assistance.

- ○ Averting eyes can indicate they do not want to be disturbed.
- ○ If a group is exchanging glances or looking toward the entrance, they may be waiting for service.

3. **Tone and Volume of Conversations**
   - ○ A lively, loud room suggests high energy and engagement.
   - ○ A quiet, subdued atmosphere may indicate a more serious or intimate setting where service should be subtle and refined.
   - ○ If you hear hushed or tense voices, there may be an issue that needs addressing discreetly.

4. **Pacing and Movement**
   - ○ Are customers moving quickly, indicating a rushed or impatient mood?
   - ○ Is there a relaxed flow to movement, suggesting a leisurely experience?
   - ○ Are employees moving with urgency or at a comfortable pace? This can affect the atmosphere and perception of service.

5. **Facial Expressions**
   - ○ Smiles, furrowed brows, or sighs, all give clues about how people are feeling.
   - ○ A customer scanning the room might be looking for assistance.
   - ○ A guest with a frustrated expression might be dissatisfied or in need of something.

Adjusting Service Based on the Room's Energy

Once you've assessed the room, the next step is adjusting your service accordingly:

- **If the energy is high and positive**, match that enthusiasm. Engage customers with an upbeat tone, be extra attentive, and ensure everyone is having a great experience.
- **If the room feels tense or rushed**, focus on efficiency. Provide quick service, anticipate needs, and offer solutions proactively.
- **If the room is quiet and intimate**, be more subtle in your approach. Use soft tones, give customers space, and ensure interactions are meaningful but not intrusive.

The Art of Intervention

Sometimes, reading a room allows you to step in before a problem escalates. Some key intervention techniques include:

- **Recognizing Frustration Early**—If a customer looks upset, check in before they need to call for assistance.
- **Managing Conflict Calmly**—If you sense tension between customers or employees, handle it discreetly and professionally.
- **Anticipating Service Needs**—If a table is looking around for a server, approach before they have to wave you down.
- **Creating Balance**—If one part of the room is too loud or overwhelming, subtly guide guests to a quieter space or adjust the environment.

Reading a Room in Different Industries

- **Hospitality:** In a restaurant, reading a room ensures you time service correctly—knowing when to check in and when to leave guests to enjoy their meal.
- **Retail:** Customers browsing with focus may not want assistance, while those looking around frequently might need help with finding something.
- **Corporate Settings:** During meetings, body language cues tell you when to speak, when to listen, and when to shift the conversation.
- **Health Care:** Understanding patient and family expressions can help caregivers provide better emotional support.

The power to read a room is an art that, once mastered, elevates your service skills to an elite level. It allows you to provide an intuitive and personalized experience, ensuring that customers feel seen, understood, and valued. By combining observation with action, you transform service from a standard process into an unforgettable experience.

The best service professionals don't just serve—they anticipate, adapt, and elevate. Reading a room is one of the most powerful tools in making service an art rather than just a function.

PART 2

Elevating the Service Experience

True service is not just about fulfilling a need; it's about elevating the experience, transforming every interaction into an opportunity to connect, delight, and leave a lasting impression.

CHAPTER 5

Beyond Transactions: Making Customers Feel Like They Belong

Bringing It All Together—The Complete Service Package

You've mastered the building blocks of exceptional service: a warm smile, a heartfelt *"How are you?,"* open and inviting body language, and the power of eye contact. Each element contributes to creating memorable experiences for your customers. Now it's time to take it one step further by focusing on the language we use—words that reinforce positivity, create connections, and make customers feel valued.

Why Language Matters

Words are powerful. They can shape perceptions, diffuse tension, and create lasting impressions. In service, your language sets the tone for interactions and communicates your attitude, enthusiasm, and willingness to help.

- **Positive Language Creates Positive Experiences:** Saying "I'd love to help" conveys excitement and readiness, while saying "I guess I can help" feels hesitant and disengaged.
- **Words Build Trust:** Clear, kind, and respectful language reassures customers that they're in good hands.
- **Language Reflects Your Brand:** Every word you say is a reflection of your service philosophy and the values of your organization.

Combining What We've Learned

Let's revisit the foundational elements of exceptional service and see how they work together when paired with positive language:

1. **A Big Welcome Smile**

   The first thing customers notice is your smile. It's the universal signal of warmth and approachability.

   - Combine this with a cheerful greeting:
     - "Good morning! It's great to see you today!"
     - "Hi there! How are you?"

   Your smile and words should feel genuine, setting a positive tone for the interaction.

2. **A Personal Connection with "How Are You?"**

   Asking "How are you?" invites the customer into a conversation, making them feel acknowledged and valued.

   - Use positive follow-ups to show attentiveness:
     - "I'm so glad to hear that! How can I assist you today?"
     - "I'm sorry to hear it's been a rough day—let me do what I can to make it better."

3. **Open and Engaged Body Language**

   Your body language reinforces your words. Standing tall, leaning slightly forward, and maintaining eye contact signal that you're present and ready to help.

   - Pair this with proactive language:
     - "I'd be happy to assist you with that."
     - "Let me walk you through your options."

4. **Eye Contact That Builds Trust**

   Eye contact shows customers they have your full attention. It enhances sincerity and makes your words more impactful.

   - Combine it with reassuring phrases:
     - "You're in great hands—I'll take care of this for you."
     - "Let's find a solution together."

The Power of Positive Language

Using positive language doesn't mean avoiding the truth or sugar-coating situations. It means framing your words in a way that focuses on solutions, possibilities, and care.

Examples of Positive Language:

- Instead of: "I don't know."
- Say: "That's a great question! Let me find out for you."
- Instead of: "We don't have that item in stock."
- Say: "That's a popular item! Let me check when it'll be available, or I can recommend something similar."
- Instead of: "You'll have to wait."
- Say: "Thank you for your patience. I'll make sure we assist you as quickly as possible."

Key Phrases to Use Often:

- "I'd be happy to help."
- "No problem at all."
- "I'd love to take care of that for you."
- "You're welcome!"
- "Thank you for giving us the opportunity to serve you."

Turning Challenges into Opportunities

Not every customer interaction will be smooth, but positive language can turn difficult situations into opportunities to build loyalty.

Scenario 1: A Customer Complaint

Customer: "This meal isn't what I ordered!"

- Response: "I'm so sorry for the mix-up! Let me take care of this right away and get you exactly what you ordered. Thank you for bringing it to my attention."

Scenario 2: A Service Delay

Customer: "I've been waiting forever!"

- Response: "I'm really sorry for the wait. I appreciate your patience, and I'll make sure you're taken care of as quickly as possible."

Training Yourself to Use Positive Language

If positive language doesn't come naturally, don't worry—it's a skill you can develop. Here are some tips:

1. **Practice Reframing Negative Phrases**
   Write down common service scenarios and brainstorm positive ways to respond. Practice these responses until they feel natural.
2. **Listen to Yourself**
   Pay attention to the words you use during interactions. Are they uplifting and solution-oriented? If not, consciously shift your phrasing.
3. **Use Role-Playing Exercises**
   Work with colleagues to practice scenarios where positive language makes a difference. Feedback can help you refine your approach.
4. **Reinforce the Habit**
   Set reminders or use sticky notes in your workspace with phrases like "I'd be happy to help" or "No problem at all."

Building Consistency as a Team

For positive language to have a lasting impact, it needs to become part of your team's culture.

- **Provide Ongoing Training:** Regularly review and practice positive phrasing during team meetings.
- **Celebrate Wins:** Recognize team members who excel in using uplifting language.
- **Lead by Example:** Managers should model positive language in their interactions with both customers and staff.

The Ultimate Service Mindset

By combining a welcoming smile, a genuine *"How are you?,"* open body language, eye contact, and positive language, you create a service experience that customers will remember. All of these elements work together to convey care, competence, and enthusiasm.

The language you use is the final piece of the puzzle, the glue that holds all the other elements together. It's your way of telling customers, *"You matter, and I'm here for you."*

As you go forward, remember that words have power. Use them wisely, and watch how they transform your service, your relationships, and your business.

The Art of Listening

In the world of exceptional service, one of the most overlooked yet powerful skills is the art of listening. Many people hear, but few truly listen. Deep listening goes beyond simply processing words—it involves understanding, interpreting, and responding in a way that makes the customer feel valued and heard. When we listen with intent, we create meaningful connections that elevate the service experience from transactional to transformational.

Why Listening Matters in Service

Every customer who walks through the door has a need, whether they explicitly state it or not. Some customers know exactly what they want, while others may be uncertain, frustrated, or even unaware of their needs. By practicing deep listening, we can uncover these needs and provide a solution that exceeds expectations.

Listening is not just about customer satisfaction—it's about customer loyalty. A customer who feels heard is more likely to return, recommend your business, and become a lifelong advocate. In contrast, a customer who feels ignored or misunderstood will quickly take their business elsewhere.

Active Listening Techniques

Active listening is a skill that requires intention and practice. Here are key techniques that service professionals can use to enhance their ability to listen effectively:

1. **Give Your Full Attention**
   Multitasking while a customer is speaking sends a clear message that their words are not important. Whether you are taking an

order, answering a question, or resolving a complaint, give the customer your full attention. Maintain eye contact, put away distractions, and be present in the moment.

2. **Use Nonverbal Cues**

   Body language plays a crucial role in effective listening. Nod occasionally to show understanding, lean in slightly to demonstrate engagement, and maintain an open posture. These small but powerful gestures signal to the customer that you are fully engaged in the conversation.

3. **Paraphrase and Confirm Understanding**

   One of the most effective ways to ensure you understand a customer's needs is by paraphrasing what they have said. For example:
   ○ Customer: "I'm looking for something quick to eat, but I have a dairy allergy."
   ○ Response: "So you're looking for a quick meal that doesn't contain dairy. Let me show you some options."

   This technique not only clarifies the customer's request but also reassures them that they have been heard.

4. **Ask Open-Ended Questions**

   Encourage customers to share more about their needs by asking open-ended questions rather than yes/no questions. Instead of asking "Do you need help with anything?" try asking "What can I do to make your visit today exceptional?" This invites the customer to open up and provides you with valuable insights.

5. **Listen for What's Not Being Said**

   Sometimes, the most important messages are unspoken. A customer's tone, hesitation, or facial expressions can reveal their emotions and needs. For example, a customer who lingers near a menu but doesn't approach may be feeling overwhelmed. Recognizing these cues allows you to step in and provide assistance before they even ask.

6. **Avoid Interrupting**

   Interrupting a customer mid-sentence not only disrupts their train of thought but also signals that what you have to say is more important than their concerns. Let the customer finish speaking before responding. This patience fosters trust and respect.

7. **Practice Reflective Listening**

Reflective listening involves repeating back key points of what the customer has said to ensure mutual understanding. For example:

- ○ Customer: "I had an issue with my last order—it was missing an item."
- ○ Response: "I understand that your last order was missing an item. I sincerely apologize for that. Let's make sure we correct this for you today."

This technique validates the customer's experience and reassures them that their concerns are being taken seriously.

The Impact of Deep Listening on Service

When service professionals master the art of deep listening, the impact is profound:

- **Increased Customer Satisfaction**: Customers feel valued when their concerns and needs are truly understood.
- **Better Problem Resolution**: Issues are resolved more effectively because the full context is considered.
- **Higher Employee Confidence**: Team members who practice deep listening are better-equipped to provide thoughtful solutions.
- **Stronger Customer Loyalty**: A customer who feels heard is more likely to return and recommend the business to others.

Real-World Examples of Listening in Service

Example 1: The Restaurant Server

A couple walks into a restaurant and mentions that they are celebrating an anniversary. A server who is actively listening takes note of this detail and later surprises them with a small complimentary dessert and a personalized note from the chef. The couple leaves with a memorable experience and is likely to return.

Example 2: The Retail Associate

A customer browsing for skincare products hesitates when asked if they need help. Instead of repeating, "Let me know if you need anything," the associate gently asks, "Are you looking for something specific today?" This subtle shift encourages the customer to share their concerns about sensitive skin, allowing the associate to offer tailored recommendations.

Example 3: The Call Center Representative

A frustrated customer calls in about a delayed order. Instead of jumping straight to a scripted apology, the representative listens attentively, acknowledges the inconvenience, and asks, "How can I make this right for you today?" By validating the customer's frustration and offering a proactive solution, the representative turns a negative experience into a positive one.

Practical Ways to Improve Your Listening Skills

If you want to refine your listening skills, try these exercises:

- **The 5-Second Rule:** Wait 5 seconds after a customer finishes speaking before responding. This ensures they have fully communicated their thoughts.
- **Mirror Conversations:** Practice paraphrasing what someone says in casual conversations to build the habit of reflective listening.
- **Daily Listening Challenge:** Challenge yourself to identify one unspoken need in each customer interaction.

The art of listening is a game-changer in service. When you truly listen, you move beyond merely serving customers—you create lasting relationships. Every interaction becomes an opportunity to connect, understand, and leave a lasting positive impression. Master this skill, and you will not only elevate your service but also create a business where customers feel valued and eager to return.

The Heart of Hospitality:
Welcoming Every Guest Like Family

Hospitality is more than a transaction—it is an experience that should make every guest feel as if they have been welcomed into the most inviting home they have ever known. True hospitality is not just about providing a service; it is about fostering an emotional connection that makes guests feel valued, respected, and genuinely cared for. When executed correctly, hospitality transforms a business from a place of commerce into a place of warmth, comfort, and belonging.

Many people in the industry see their job as providing a service—taking orders, delivering food, making drinks, or offering assistance. However, hospitality requires a fundamental shift in mindset. Instead of viewing guests as customers, think of them as **honored guests in your home.** Imagine how you would welcome a respected friend or an esteemed colleague into your personal space. Would you simply serve them and walk away, or would you go above and beyond to ensure their experience was exceptional?

This is the heart of hospitality—treating each guest as if they are the most important person you will welcome that day. It is about making people feel seen, heard, and appreciated in a way that lingers long after they leave.

When guests walk through the doors of a hospitality establishment, they should feel an immediate sense of comfort and familiarity. This feeling does not come from the physical space alone—it is created by the people within it. Every member of the team plays a role in setting the tone for the guest experience. Warmth in greetings, attentiveness in service, and sincerity in interactions, all contribute to making guests feel as though they are returning to a home they love.

Consider the details that make a house feel like a home—the welcoming smile of a host, the offer of a seat, and the way someone takes the time to learn preferences and anticipate needs. In a hospitality setting, these same elements should be at play. **It is about creating a space where guests do not just feel accommodated; they feel like they belong.**

Recognition and Personalization: The Secret to Lasting Loyalty

One of the most powerful ways to elevate hospitality is through recognition and personalization. We have talked a lot about this throughout the book; however, it is your secret weapon. Regular guests should be acknowledged with genuine enthusiasm. Remembering a favorite drink order, preferred seating area, or special occasion makes a profound impact. Personalization goes beyond knowing a name—it is about making someone feel truly valued.

When guests return to a place and are greeted with warmth and familiarity, they feel a deep connection to the establishment. It fosters a sense of loyalty that no marketing campaign or discount offer can replicate. This is why businesses that master hospitality build lasting relationships with their customers.

Welcoming Guests Like the Most Respected Person You Know

Imagine that someone you deeply respect and admire—whether a mentor, a loved one, or a public figure—was walking into your establishment. How would you greet them? What extra steps would you take to ensure they had a remarkable experience? Would you not ask them how they are? This is the level of care that should be extended to **every single guest.**

- Would you rush through their order without eye contact? Or would you take the time to engage with them, making them feel truly important?
- Would you allow their space to be untidy or uncomfortable? Or would you ensure every detail was perfect, just as you would in your own home?

When teams embrace this mindset, service transcends routine tasks. It becomes a powerful act of making people feel valued and welcome, every single time.

In a world where consumers have endless choices, businesses that master hospitality hold a distinct competitive advantage. Price and product alone are no longer enough to build loyalty—**people remember how they were made to feel.** The businesses that make guests feel like family will always have the upper hand over those that treat interactions as mere transactions.

As the cost of living rises, so do customer expectations. When people choose to spend their hard-earned money, they want more than just a product or service—they want an experience that justifies their investment. Businesses that provide **exceptional hospitality** will not only survive but in fact thrive, as guests return time and time again for the feeling they create.

Hospitality is an art that requires dedication, consistency, and a deep understanding of human connection. It is about making every guest feel like they are stepping into a home where they are respected, valued, and truly welcome. When this mindset becomes the foundation of a business, success follows naturally.

By embracing hospitality as more than service—as an opportunity to create lasting impressions—you set your business apart in a profound way. Guests will return not just for what you offer but, more importantly, for how you make them feel. **And that is the true power of hospitality.**

The Little Touches That Make a Big Difference

In the world of hospitality, the smallest gestures often have the most profound impact. Service is not just about meeting basic expectations; it's about exceeding them in subtle, meaningful ways. The feeling of being truly welcomed—of being seen, acknowledged, and valued—creates a lasting impression that turns a one-time visitor into a lifelong customer. These little touches, though seemingly insignificant, are the building blocks of loyalty and exceptional service.

1. **A Handwritten Note for Special Occasions**
   Instead of just acknowledging a birthday or anniversary verbally, imagine placing a small handwritten note on the table thanking the guest for celebrating their special moment at your establishment. A personal touch like this, written by the manager or a team member, makes them feel valued and seen.

Example:

"Happy Anniversary, James & Sarah! We're honored to be part of your celebration tonight. Wishing you many more years of love and happiness!"

2. **Welcoming a First-Time Guest Like an Old Friend**

   When a new guest dines with you, ensure multiple team members make them feel like part of the family. After the initial greeting, pass their name and details along to the supervisor or another team member. Throughout the meal, they receive warm, genuine acknowledgments that reinforce their importance.

   Example:

   "Hi Mark, I heard it's your first time dining with us! We're so happy to have you here—how's everything so far?"

   The key is to make them feel recognized without overwhelming them. This technique ensures they leave feeling like they belong and return as a regular.

3. **Personalized Farewell and Invitation to Return**

   Most restaurants and cafés offer a standard "Thank you for coming," but imagine a farewell that's personal and inviting. If a guest has been in for breakfast and mentions they're in town for work, a staff member could say:

   Example:

   "We loved having you for breakfast today, Emma! If you need a great lunch spot later, we'd love to see you again."

   It creates an open-ended invitation that feels warm and intentional rather than generic.

4. **Unexpected Complimentary Gesture Based on the Conversation**

   If a guest mentions that they've just come from a long flight, imagine offering them a complimentary tea or a small piece of short-bread to accompany their coffee, acknowledging their journey.

   Example:

   "You must be exhausted after such a long flight. Let me bring you a calming herbal tea—on the house. It's our little way of saying welcome."

   These spontaneous gestures feel organic and heartfelt, rather than scripted promotions.

5. **Celebrating Milestones for Regulars**

   For returning guests, keeping track of small milestones—such as a 10th visit—can be an incredible way to show appreciation. When a customer hits a milestone, offer them a handwritten thank-you card or a small surprise.

   Example:

   "John, we just realized this is your 10th visit with us! Thank you for being part of our family—we appreciate you!"

   It's an effortless way to reinforce loyalty while making customers feel valued beyond transactions.

Make Customers Feel Like They Belong

When a customer walks into your business, they are stepping into your world. They may be visiting for the first time or returning for the hundredth, but one thing remains the same: They want to feel welcomed, valued, and comfortable. The most successful businesses are the ones that create a sense of belonging, where customers don't just feel like guests—they feel like they're home.

Belonging is a powerful emotion. It's the feeling of being seen, understood, and appreciated. In hospitality and customer service, this emotional connection is what transforms one-time visitors into lifelong regulars. It's what makes people rave about their experience, not just for the food or the service but, more importantly, for how they felt.

This section explores how to create that feeling of belonging, the small but meaningful actions that make customers feel part of something special, and how a welcoming environment fosters deep loyalty.

1. **The Psychology of Belonging in Customer Service**

   Humans crave connection. Studies show that feeling a sense of belonging can increase happiness, reduce stress, and even impact purchasing decisions. When customers feel at home in your business, they stay longer, spend more, and return more frequently.

   Think about your favorite café or restaurant. What makes you go back? It's not just the coffee or the menu—it's the way you're treated, the familiarity, the feeling that you matter. Customers want that experience, and businesses that provide it create an emotional connection that competitors can't easily replicate.

Belonging isn't about grand gestures—it's about consistent, thoughtful actions that make people feel like part of a community.

Creating a sense of belonging isn't just a feel-good strategy—it has measurable business benefits. According to research published in *Harvard Business Review*, customers who feel emotionally connected to a brand are more than twice as valuable as those who are simply satisfied (Magids et al. 2015). These emotionally engaged customers tend to visit more frequently, spend more per visit, and show greater brand loyalty—even when competitors offer similar products or services. This makes the case clear: When businesses cultivate an environment where people feel truly valued and at home, they build not just repeat business but also become long-term brand advocates.

2. **Creating a Sense of Belonging from the First Interaction**
   The way a customer is greeted sets the tone for their entire experience. The first few moments determine whether they feel welcomed or feel like just another transaction.
   - **A Warm, Personalized Welcome**—A simple "Welcome back, Tom! Great to see you again!" instantly makes a returning customer feel like they belong. If it's a new customer, a warm "We're so glad you're here! Is this your first time with us?" opens the door for connection.
   - **Recognizing New Guests**—If a customer is visiting for the first time, ensuring multiple team members check in with them can make them feel like their presence matters.
   - **Noticing the Small Details**—If a customer walks in carrying a shopping bag, acknowledging it with a friendly "Done some shopping today?" creates an immediate personal connection.

3. **The Little Things That Make a Big Difference**
   Creating a sense of belonging isn't about big discounts or promotions—it's about the small, thoughtful details that make customers feel valued.
   - **Remembering Names and Preferences**—There's a reason why people return to places where they're remembered. If a customer

always orders a particular coffee, having a barista say, "The usual today, Sarah?" makes them feel like they belong.

- ○ **Celebrating Small Milestones**—Acknowledging a customer's 10th visit with a small "Thanks for being part of our family!" note can create an emotional bond.
- ○ **Providing Unexpected Extras**—If a regular guest always sits by the window, keeping that table open for them when possible makes them feel considered and valued.

4. **Creating a "Home Away from Home" Atmosphere**
   Customers should feel like they're stepping into a place where they are truly wanted. This requires a mindset shift—seeing every guest as a valued part of the business rather than just another transaction.

   - ○ **Consistency Is Key**—Customers should receive the same warm experience regardless of who serves them. The team should be trained to maintain a welcoming, positive atmosphere at all times.
   - ○ **Genuine Conversations**—Encouraging natural, friendly interactions makes customers feel comfortable. A simple "How was your day?" can start meaningful connections.
   - ○ **A Community Feeling**—Hosting small events, remembering customer birthdays, or just creating a space where people feel at ease help turn a business into a second home.

5. **Handling Complaints with Care**
   Even when things go wrong, businesses that make customers feel valued can turn a negative experience into a loyalty-building moment.

   - ○ **Apologizing with Sincerity**—Customers don't just want a problem solved; they want to feel heard. A heartfelt statement, "I'm so sorry that happened. Let me make it right for you," can go a long way.
   - ○ **Following Up**—If a regular customer has had an issue, following up on their next visit with "I really appreciate you coming back—thank you" reinforces their importance.

6. **Making Every Customer Feel Like They Belong, Every Time**
   At the heart of it all, making customers feel like they belong is about treating them with the same warmth and respect as you would a guest in your home.

When a business consistently makes customers feel valued, appreciated, and welcomed, they don't just gain customers—they gain loyal supporters who return time and time again, not just for the service but, instead, for the feeling of belonging.

The Power of the Checkback

The checkback is one of the simplest yet most powerful tools in customer service. Done correctly, it enhances the guest experience, ensures satisfaction, and provides an opportunity to correct any issues before they escalate. Despite its importance, many businesses overlook or rush this step, missing the chance to strengthen customer relationships.

A well-executed checkback shows that the business values its customers and their experience. It reassures them that they are not just another order number but a valued guest whose experience matters. Whether in hospitality, retail, or any customer-facing industry, mastering the art of the checkback can be the difference between a forgettable visit and one that turns a first-time guest into a loyal customer.

1. **The Psychology Behind the Checkback**
   Customers want to feel valued. A checkback reassures them that their experience matters and that they are being looked after.
   1.1 Why the Checkback Works:
   - **It provides reassurance.** Customers feel confident knowing someone is paying attention to their experience.
   - **It builds trust.** A proactive checkback shows that a business cares, rather than waiting for complaints.
   - **It improves overall satisfaction.** When customers are given a chance to provide feedback mid-experience, they leave happier because they know their needs were considered.
   1.2 Emotional Impact:
   - A well-timed checkback **creates a connection.** It turns a transactional experience into a personal one.
   - Customers feel **heard and respected**, strengthening their positive perception of the business.
   - It prevents dissatisfaction from escalating into frustration or complaints.

2. **Timing the Checkback: When and How to Do It Right**
   2.1 The Ideal Timing
   The best checkbacks are well-timed, meaning they don't interrupt but come at a moment when they add value. Here's how it applies in different settings:
   2.2 In Hospitality (Restaurants, Cafés, and Hotels):
   - **After the first few bites or sips:** Checking in too soon means the customer hasn't had a chance to assess the food. Too late, and they may have already decided not to return.
   - **Midway through the meal:** If a guest seems to be slowing down, it's an opportunity to check if they need anything else.
   - **Before finishing:** This allows the server to upsell (desserts, another drink) or ensure the meal has been enjoyable.

   2.3 In Retail or Service-Based Businesses:
   - **Shortly after a customer starts browsing or trying a product:** A gentle check-in such as "Let me know if you have any questions" allows engagement without pressure.
   - **Midway through a service (salons, auto shops, and personal consultations):** Asking how things are going reassures the customer that their needs are a priority.
   - **Post-purchase follow-up:** Sending an e-mail or calling a customer to check on a product/service adds an extra layer of care.

   2.4 How to Execute It Well
   - **Approach with confidence but with warmth.** A smile and direct eye contact make the checkback feel genuine.
   - **Use open-ended questions.** Instead of a generic "Everything okay?" try "How is everything so far?" or "Is there anything I can do to make this better?"
   - **Be available but not intrusive.** Gauge the customer's body language—if they seem engaged in conversation, keep it brief.

3. **Reading Customer Cues: The Art of Adjusting Your Checkback**
   A checkback is not a one-size-fits-all approach. Different customers require different levels of engagement.
   3.1 Types of Customers and How to Check Back
   1. **The Engaged Customer**
      - They make eye contact, respond positively, and seem open to conversation.

- **Approach**: Be more personal—engage in light conversation while checking in.

2. **The Reserved Customer**
   - They answer briefly or nod but don't engage further.
   - **Approach**: Keep it short and professional.

3. **The Dissatisfied Customer (Without Complaining Yet)**
   - Signs include pushing food around the plate, checking the bill early, or looking around frequently.
   - **Approach**: Check in subtly but be ready to offer a solution. "I noticed you haven't had much of your meal. Can I bring something else?"

3.2 Nonverbal Cues to Watch For

○ **Nods and smiles:** They're satisfied and engaged.

○ **Avoiding eye contact and crossed arms:** They may have concerns but don't want to voice them immediately.

○ **Looking around or glancing at staff:** They might need something but don't know how to ask.

4. **Common Mistakes and How to Avoid Them**

   4.1 The Five Most Common Checkback Mistakes

   1. **The robotic checkback**—Asking "Everything okay?" without real engagement sounds impersonal.
      - **Fix:** Personalize it—"Is the steak cooked to your liking?" or "Are you enjoying the wine selection?"

   2. **Checking in too late**—By the time you ask, it's too late to fix anything.
      - **Fix:** Time it earlier in the experience but not immediately after serving.

   3. **Interrupting at the wrong moment**—If a customer is deep in conversation or mid-bite, it feels intrusive.
      - **Fix:** Observe before approaching—Find a natural break.

   4. **Not acting on feedback**—If a customer mentions something is off, but nothing is done, the checkback loses its value.
      - **Fix:** Act immediately or acknowledge their feedback genuinely.

5. **Overdoing it**—Too many check-ins can feel like micromanagement.

   ▪ **Fix:** Balance attentiveness with giving the customer space.

5. **Problem Resolution and Recovery Through the Checkback**

   One of the most valuable aspects of the checkback is its ability to fix issues before they escalate.

   5.1 How a Checkback Can Save a Customer's Experience

   Imagine a guest at a restaurant finds their steak overcooked but hesitates to complain. If a server checks in and asks, "Is the steak cooked the way you like it?" the guest now has a chance to voice their concern. The issue is fixed before they leave unhappy.

   5.2 Key Steps in Problem Recovery:

   1. **Acknowledge the concern immediately**—"I'm really sorry about that. Let me take care of it for you."

   2. **Offer a solution without hesitation**—Replace, adjust, or provide an alternative.

   3. **Follow up again**—"Is everything better now? I really appreciate your patience."

   4. **End on a positive note**—Thank them for allowing you to make it right.

6. **Elevating Customer Loyalty Through the Checkback**

   Customers remember how they felt. A great checkback leaves them feeling valued and cared for.

   6.1 How to Use the Checkback to Build Loyalty:

   ○ Make regular guests feel special by remembering their preferences.

   ○ For new customers, use the checkback to create a welcoming first impression.

   ○ If a customer has an issue, following up on their next visit shows genuine commitment to service.

   Businesses that master the checkback don't just provide good service—they create memorable experiences that keep customers returning.

Conclusion: Making the Checkback a Nonnegotiable

The checkback is a simple but powerful habit that separates good service from exceptional service. It prevents problems, strengthens customer relationships, and builds loyalty.

When done with warmth, attentiveness, and sincerity, it ensures that every customer leaves with a positive memory—one that brings them back again and again.

CHAPTER 6

The Little Things That Make a Big Difference

Service is about meeting needs. Hospitality, however, is about making people feel at home. While service ensures that a customer receives what they ask for, hospitality creates an experience that makes them want to return. It's not simply about fulfilling a transaction or delivering a product; it's about the way people feel during and after their interaction with a business. True hospitality nurtures a sense of belonging, comfort, and appreciation. It goes beyond the basic expectations of service, making each individual feel genuinely cared for. This section is not just for the hospitality industry but applies across all sectors, showing how these principles can be adapted and applied in any environment where people interact with a business.

Hospitality is about crafting experiences—transforming the ordinary into something extraordinary. It's about recognizing that every interaction with a customer or client is an opportunity to build a relationship. This is why hospitality is not confined to the hospitality industry alone. Every industry uses the core principles of hospitality, even if it's not always recognized. Whether you work in health care, retail, education, or corporate environments, hospitality is embedded in how we connect with others. The definition of hospitality, by dictionary standards, is "the friendly and generous reception and entertainment of guests, visitors, or strangers." It's about making others feel welcome and valued, no matter the setting.

Think of the last time you visited a café, hotel, or even a retail store and left feeling genuinely cared for. What made that experience stand out? Was it the warmth in the greeting, the attention to detail, or the way the team anticipated your needs before you even voiced them? These are the elements of hospitality that transform a simple transaction into something meaningful. It's in the small things: the barista who remembers your order, the store associate who takes a moment to offer assistance, the receptionist who greets you with a smile that makes you feel comfortable. These moments create a feeling that lasts well beyond the interaction.

Hospitality is not just for restaurants or hotels—it applies to any business that interacts with customers. A well-trained retail associate can make a customer feel as welcome as a host in a five-star resort. A receptionist at a corporate office can extend the same level of care as a concierge in a luxury hotel. In fact, it's often these industries, where the focus might not traditionally be on "service," that benefit the most from incorporating hospitality principles. The principles of hospitality transcend industry boundaries, and those who master it gain a competitive edge that cannot be replicated by price or convenience alone. A hospital receptionist who makes a patient feel at ease or a car service professional who takes extra time to explain the work done, both create lasting impressions that build trust and loyalty.

The mindset that separates hospitality from service: Service is about meeting a need, but hospitality is about going beyond that to create an emotional connection.

The small but powerful gestures that create lasting impressions: How little things—like a warm smile, remembering a customer's preferences, or showing empathy—can make a significant difference.

How to make every guest feel like they belong: The importance of making each individual feel valued and seen, whether they are a first-time customer or a regular.

Hospitality is an art—one that requires skill, awareness, and a commitment to exceeding expectations. It's about anticipating needs before they are voiced, listening with intention, and providing care and attention that makes others feel welcome. Hospitality isn't just about creating a comfortable environment; it's about cultivating a positive and memorable experience that customers will cherish and want to return to. Let's explore how to master it and elevate the customer experience to something unforgettable, no matter the industry or context. The principles of hospitality have the power to transform any business by turning customers into loyal advocates, creating an atmosphere where people don't just come for the service but mainly because they feel at home.

The Power of Giving Your Name and "I Will Be Looking After You"

In any customer-facing role, the first impression sets the tone for the entire interaction. One of the most powerful yet often overlooked elements of a great first impression is **introducing yourself by name and personally taking responsibility for the guest's experience**.

When a server, receptionist, concierge, or team member says, **"Hi, I'm Sarah, and I'll be looking after you today,"** it immediately creates a connection. It makes the interaction **human**, shifts the dynamic from a transactional exchange to a relationship, and gives the guest confidence that someone is personally invested in their satisfaction.

This small act can:

- **Build trust and comfort.**
- **Create accountability and a sense of responsibility.**
- **Make service feel more personal and welcoming.**
- **Encourage guests to engage and communicate their needs.**
- **Turn a routine experience into a memorable one.**

This section will explore **why giving your name matters**, how to deliver it effectively, and how it transforms the hospitality and service industries.

The Psychology Behind Sharing Your Name

A name is more than just a label—it's an invitation for connection. When you introduce yourself, you **humanize the interaction** and make the guest feel **personally cared for** rather than just being another customer.

Why This Works

1. **It Creates a** Personal **Connection**
   - Guests feel more comfortable addressing a real person rather than an anonymous employee.
   - They are more likely to communicate their preferences and needs.

2. **It Builds Trust and Accountability**
   - When you give your name, you're **taking ownership** of their experience.
   - Guests feel reassured that there's someone who is personally responsible for them.

3. **It Reduces Complaints and Enhances Feedback**
   - Guests are more likely to voice concerns politely when they see you as a person rather than just "the staff."
   - They feel safe asking for adjustments instead of silently leaving dissatisfied.

4. **It Encourages Repeat Visits and Loyalty**
   - People remember positive interactions with **individuals**, not just businesses.
   - When guests return and are greeted by name, they feel like they **belong.**

How to Introduce Yourself Effectively

While the act of giving your name is simple, **how** you deliver it makes all the difference.

The Perfect Introduction Formula

1. **Make eye contact and smile.** This shows confidence and warmth.
2. **Use a friendly, natural tone.** Avoid sounding robotic or rehearsed.
3. **Say your name and your role.** Example:
   - "Hi, I'm Emily, and I'll be looking after you today."
   - "Good evening, I'm Jake, and I'll be your server for tonight."
4. **Add a welcoming phrase.** Example:
   - "If there's anything I can do to make your experience better, just let me know."
   - "It's great to have you here! Let me know if you need anything."
5. **Engage with the guest's name if possible.** If they introduce themselves or if you see their name on a reservation, use it:
   - "Welcome, Mr. Johnson! It's a pleasure to have you here today."

Small Actions That Reinforce the Personal Touch

Introducing yourself is just the beginning. To **fully utilize** the power of personal service, follow through with small actions that show you truly care.

Five Small Yet Powerful Actions to Reinforce Connection

1. **Remember One Detail About the Guest**
   - If they mention it's their birthday, anniversary, or a special occasion, acknowledge it later.
   - Example: "How's the birthday celebration going so far, James?"
2. **Check Back Using Your Name**
   - Instead of just asking, "Is everything okay?" say, **"James, just checking in—Is everything to your liking?"**
   - This reinforces the personal connection and keeps the conversation warm.
3. **Follow Up with a Personalized Farewell**
   - If they mentioned it was their first time visiting, say:
     "It was a pleasure serving you today, Mr. Johnson. I hope you enjoyed your first visit, and I'd love to see you again soon!"
   - If they are a regular: **"Great seeing you again, Sarah! Looking forward to next time."**
4. **Offer a Small Personalized Gesture**
   - If a guest says they love a certain drink or dessert, acknowledge it:
     "I remember you love our chai lattes—I've got one coming right up!"
   - If they mention they are in a hurry, adjust accordingly:
     "I'll have the bill ready as soon as you're finished so you're not rushed."
5. **Introduce Other Team Members by Name**
   - "If you need anything while I'm away, my colleague Jake will be happy to assist you."
   - This makes the guest feel **continually looked after** even if shifts change.

Overcoming Barriers: Why Some Employees Avoid Giving Their Name

Some employees hesitate to introduce themselves because they:

- Feel uncomfortable putting themselves in the spotlight.
- Worry about personal accountability if something goes wrong.
- Aren't used to this level of engagement with customers.

How to Encourage Team Members to Adopt This Habit

- **Practice in team meetings.** Role-play introductions until it feels natural.
- **Reinforce that giving your name builds confidence, not vulnerability.** Guests see you as more professional and capable.
- **Remind them that it makes their job easier.** A warm introduction leads to **happier customers** and **fewer difficult interactions**.

The Impact of Using Names in Different Industries

Hospitality (Hotels, Restaurants, Cafés)

- Guests feel a personal **attachment** to the business.
- They are more likely to return because they feel **recognized and valued**.
- Complaints are reduced because guests feel comfortable bringing up concerns **early on**.

Retail

- A simple **"Hi, I'm Lily, let me know if I can help with anything"** makes the customer feel **welcome rather than pressured**.
- It increases engagement, making people more likely to **browse longer and purchase more**.

Health Care and Wellness

- Patients feel safer and more **emotionally connected** to their care provider.
- Saying, **"Hi, I'm Dr. Patel, and I'll be taking care of you today,"** builds **instant trust**.

Corporate and Customer Service

- Phone agents who say, **"Hi, my name is Alex, and I'll be assisting you today,"** create an immediate sense of **care and professionalism**.
- Customers feel **less frustration** when they know exactly who is helping them.

The Long-Term Benefits: Why This Small Habit Transforms Customer Loyalty

Why This Creates Repeat Customers

1. **Memorable interactions:** Customers remember and return to places where they feel personally connected.
2. **Increased trust:** Guests know someone is **taking care of them**, making them more likely to spend more and come back.
3. **More positive reviews:** People share stories of **personalized, warm service**.
4. **Stronger team engagement:** When staff members take ownership of guest experiences, service naturally improves across the board.

At the heart of hospitality is **human connection**. A name is a powerful tool—it transforms a faceless interaction into a **relationship**.

By introducing yourself, taking ownership, and reinforcing that personal touch throughout the experience, you **create lasting guest loyalty** and **turn one-time customers into lifelong fans**.

CHAPTER 7

The Power of Gratitude: Thank You and Follow-Through

Following Through with Gratitude: The Power of a Thank You That Lasts

In the world of service, expressing gratitude is a cornerstone of building meaningful connections with customers. A simple "thank you" goes a long way, but the real magic happens when you follow through with your thank you—when you show that your gratitude extends beyond words into genuine actions.

A thank-you is more than a social nicety; it's a way to acknowledge someone's choice to engage with your business. Whether they've spent their time, money, or attention, showing gratitude is your opportunity to make them feel valued and appreciated. Research supports the idea that gratitude, when followed by genuine actions, builds emotional bonds that go beyond a single transaction. According to a study published in the *Journal of Consumer Psychology*, thanking customers sincerely and personalizing their experience foster satisfaction and encourage them to return, refer others, and speak positively about the business. This emotional connection transforms everyday interactions into powerful, loyalty-building moments.

The Three Pillars of an Impactful Thank-You

1. **Sincerity**: A genuine thank-you is heartfelt and specific.
2. **Reinforcement**: Follow-through ensures your words are matched by actions.
3. **Connection**: Gratitude fosters a deeper bond, turning a transactional interaction into a relational one.

The Follow-Through: Beyond Words

Saying thank you is the starting point, but following-through is where the magic happens. This means taking extra steps to show your gratitude in ways that resonate with the customer.

Examples of Thank-You Follow-Through:

1. **Personalized Notes**
   After a customer visits, send a thank-you card or e-mail. Mention something specific about their visit, such as the product they purchased or the special occasion they celebrated.
   - **Impact**: Personalization makes customers feel seen and remembered.

2. **Surprise Offers**
   Reward loyal customers with unexpected perks, like a discount, a free item, or early access to a new product.
   - **Impact**: A thoughtful gesture reinforces your gratitude and encourages repeat business.

3. **Check-Ins**
   If a customer raises a concern or purchases a product requiring support, follow up to ensure satisfaction.
   - **Example**: "Thank you for choosing our service. I wanted to check in and make sure everything is working well for you."
   - **Impact**: Follow-ups show you care about their experience beyond the sale.

4. **Public Recognition**
   Highlight loyal customers or positive reviews in your business's communications, like newsletters or social media posts.
   - **Impact**: Publicly expressing gratitude shows appreciation while fostering community.

Gratitude is a powerful emotion, and when customers feel truly appreciated, it triggers positive associations with your business. This emotional connection can lead to the following:

1. **Increased Loyalty**
   A follow-through thank-you encourages repeat visits and long-term relationships.

2. **Word-of-Mouth Marketing**

   Grateful customers are more likely to share their positive experiences with others.

3. **Higher Satisfaction**

   Feeling valued improves overall customer satisfaction, even if minor issues arise.

Practical Tips for Following Through

1. **Be Timely**

   Timing is critical. Follow up with your thank-you as soon as possible to keep the sentiment fresh.

   ○ **Example**: Send a thank-you e-mail within 24 hours of a visit or purchase.

2. **Be Specific**

   Generic gratitude feels impersonal. Reference details unique to the customer or their experience.

   ○ **Example**: "Thank you for celebrating your anniversary with us. It was an honor to be part of such a special day."

3. **Be Consistent**

   Gratitude should be a regular part of your service routine, not an occasional effort.

   ○ **Example**: Train your team to end every interaction with a genuine thank-you.

4. **Add a Personal Touch**

   Tailor your thank-you to the individual. This could mean addressing them by name, referencing a previous interaction, or offering something tailored to their preferences.

   ○ **Example**: "We're so grateful for your continued support, Sarah. Your feedback on our new menu items has been invaluable."

Transformative Stories of Follow-Through Gratitude

1. **A Coffee Shop's Loyalty Boost**

   A café started sending handwritten thank-you notes to customers who purchased loyalty cards. Within months, cardholders increased their visits and began recommending the café to friends.

2. **The Restaurant That Remembered**

   A dining restaurant implemented a system to log details about repeat customers, such as favorite dishes or special occasions. Thank-
   you e-mails referencing these details created a surge in customer
   loyalty.

3. **A Retailer's Surprise Gesture**

   An online boutique began including a small thank-you gift with
   orders, such as a handwritten card or a sample product. Customers frequently shared their delight on social media, driving brand
   awareness.

Overcoming Challenges with Gratitude Follow-Through

1. **Scaling Efforts in Larger Businesses**

   In large-scale operations, personalized follow-ups can seem
   daunting.
   Solution: Use technology, like CRM software, to automate
   follow-ups while maintaining a personal touch.

2. **Balancing Time Constraints**

   Following up with every customer can feel overwhelming in busy
   environments.
   Solution: Focus on high-impact opportunities, such as first-time
   visitors, large purchases, or resolving complaints.

3. **Ensuring Team Buy-In**

   Not everyone on your team may see the value of gratitude
   follow-through.
   Solution: Train your team on the benefits of this practice and share
   success stories to inspire them.

Simple Phrases to Reinforce Gratitude

The language of your thank-you matters. Use phrases that express sincerity and reinforce appreciation:

- "We're so glad you chose us today."
- "Thank you for spending your time with us—it means the world."

- "It was such a pleasure to serve you."
- "We're grateful for your support. Please let us know how we can continue to serve you."

Measuring the Impact of Gratitude Follow-Through

To assess how your follow-up efforts are making a difference, consider these metrics:

1. **Customer Retention Rates**
   Track whether customers return more frequently after receiving a thank-you.
2. **Feedback and Reviews**
   Monitor customer feedback to identify mentions of follow-up gestures.
3. **Referrals**
   Measure the increase in referrals, as loyal and appreciated customers often spread the word.

A thank-you is a powerful tool, but following through with it takes your service to the next level. By reinforcing your gratitude with genuine actions, you transform customer interactions into lasting relationships.

Every thank-you is an opportunity to show customers that they're more than a transaction—they're valued, appreciated, and integral to your success. So go the extra mile, follow through, and watch as gratitude reshapes your business, one thank-you at a time.

CHAPTER 8

Handling Complaints and Turning Problems into Opportunities

Handling Difficult Customers with Grace

No matter how excellent your service is, difficult customer interactions are inevitable. The real test of great service is not avoiding complaints, but handling them with professionalism, empathy, and grace. This chapter will focus on strategies for managing tense situations, defusing conflicts, and turning negative experiences into positive ones, all while incorporating the service principles we have covered—eye contact, empathy, body language, and authenticity.

The Importance of Staying Composed

The first step in handling a difficult customer is maintaining your composure. Customers can sense frustration or defensiveness, and it often escalates the situation further. By staying calm, maintaining a steady voice, and demonstrating an open posture, you create an environment where the customer feels heard and respected.

Strategies for Dealing with Complaints

1. **Make Immediate Eye Contact**—Looking the customer in the eyes signals that you are paying full attention and that their concerns matter.
2. **Listen with Empathy**—Let them express their frustration before responding. Use phrases like, "I can see why this would be frustrating for you."

3. **Use Open and Positive Body Language**—Avoid crossing your arms or looking away. Nodding slightly and leaning in shows engagement.

4. **Validate Their Feelings**—Sometimes, customers just want to be heard. A simple acknowledgment of their concerns—"I understand where you're coming from"—can go a long way.

5. **Avoid Immediate Defensiveness**—Even if the customer is wrong, resisting the urge to correct them immediately helps prevent unnecessary escalation.

6. **Use Their Name**—Personalization creates a connection. "I appreciate your patience, Sarah. Let's work on a solution together."

7. **Offer a Clear Solution**—Rather than just apologizing, take actionable steps to resolve the issue: "Here's what I can do for you."

8. **Follow-Up**—If possible, check in later to ensure the customer is satisfied with the resolution. This can be a simple phone call or e-mail.

Turning a Negative into a Positive

Great service professionals see complaints as opportunities. Handling an issue well can convert a frustrated customer into a loyal one.

- **Surprise and Delight**—Going the extra mile, like offering a small discount, a free coffee, or a handwritten note, can completely shift the customer's perception.

- **Show Authenticity**—Avoid scripted apologies. Instead of "I'm sorry for the inconvenience," try "I really appreciate your patience, and I want to make this right for you." There is a simple powerful statement that goes a long way, "It is important to me that you leave here today happy."

- **Encourage Your Team to Take Ownership**—Empowering the team to resolve issues creatively strengthens customer trust and ensures a seamless experience.

A single bad interaction can spread quickly through word-of-mouth or online reviews, but an exceptional recovery story can turn an unhappy customer into an ambassador for your brand. By using the skills we've covered—eye contact, empathy, body language, positive language, and authenticity—you can handle even the most difficult customers with confidence and care.

Great service goes beyond simply responding to what a customer says on the surface. It requires us to ask why. Why is this customer feeling this way? And then ask why again. This process of digging deeper helps us uncover the true emotions beneath their words, emotions that often drive their frustration or dissatisfaction. It is important to remember that while a customer's facts or perceptions might sometimes be inaccurate, their feelings are always real and valid. Validating those feelings does not mean agreeing with every detail. It means acknowledging their experience as genuine and worthy of respect. When we honor the emotions behind the complaint with empathy and curiosity, we create space for real connection and understanding. This approach not only helps to de-escalate conflict but also builds trust and loyalty. It embodies the core principles of excellent service, such as eye contact, empathy, body language, and authenticity that we have explored throughout this chapter. By embracing this mindset, we transform challenging interactions from obstacles into opportunities to serve with humanity and integrity. Great service isn't about never making mistakes; it's about how you handle them when they happen.

The Power of Empathy

Empathy is one of the most powerful tools in service. It goes beyond simply providing a product or completing a transaction; it is about truly understanding and connecting with customers. When we approach service with empathy, we create experiences that are meaningful and lasting.

At its core, empathy is the ability to put yourself in someone else's shoes. It means understanding what a customer is feeling, anticipating their needs, and responding with kindness and sincerity. Customers want to feel heard, understood, and valued, and empathy allows us to provide that in every interaction.

Empathy can take many forms in service. It might be as simple as recognizing when a customer is having a rough day and offering a kind word. It could be going the extra mile to accommodate a special request or being patient when a customer is confused or frustrated. Small acts of empathy can transform an ordinary experience into an extraordinary one.

One of the most common places where empathy plays a crucial role is in handling complaints or difficult situations. When a customer is upset, our natural reaction might be to defend ourselves or the business. However, approaching the situation with empathy shifts the focus from proving a point to understanding the customer's frustration. Instead of saying, "That's our policy," we can say, "I completely understand how frustrating that must be. Let me see how I can help." This small shift in language makes a world of difference.

Empathy is not a soft skill; it is a strategic imperative. When organizations consistently demonstrate genuine care by listening attentively, responding thoughtfully, and recognizing the human behind the customer, they cultivate trust and deepen loyalty. Clients are not merely retained; they are engaged, invested, and far more likely to advocate for brands that treat them with dignity and understanding. In today's service landscape, empathy is not optional; it is essential.

Active listening is a key component of empathy. Customers want to feel heard, and sometimes, simply listening to them without interrupting or rushing them can resolve an issue. Nodding, maintaining eye contact, and responding with phrases like "I understand" or "That sounds frustrating" can show that we are engaged and truly care.

Empathy also plays a role in anticipating customer needs. Have you ever noticed a customer struggling to carry their tray and offered to help? Have you seen someone looking lost and approached them before they had to ask for assistance? These are small but significant examples of how empathy enhances the service experience.

Beyond individual interactions, empathy should be ingrained in a company's culture. When businesses prioritize empathy, they foster a work environment where employees feel supported, leading to better service. When employees feel valued, they naturally extend that same care to customers.

Training teams to be empathetic doesn't require elaborate programs. It starts with simple reminders to treat every customer as a human being with their own struggles, joys, and expectations. Encouraging staff to pause and consider what the customer might be experiencing helps them respond with patience and kindness.

Empathy in service is also about inclusivity. Recognizing that customers come from different backgrounds, have different abilities, and may have unique needs allows businesses to provide thoughtful and personalized experiences. Whether it's offering assistance to an elderly customer, being mindful of dietary restrictions, or accommodating language barriers, these efforts make a business stand out.

One of the most remarkable things about empathy is that it fosters trustworthiness. Customers remember businesses that made them feel cared for. They return not just because of the product or service but because of the way they were treated. A simple act of kindness can turn a one-time visitor into a lifelong customer.

To cultivate empathy in service, we must:

- Actively listen to customers and validate their concerns.
- Use language that acknowledges and supports rather than dismisses.
- Anticipate needs and offer help before being asked.
- Approach complaints with a mindset of resolution and understanding.
- Foster a work culture where employees feel valued, so they pass that care on to customers.
- Be mindful of diverse needs and ensure inclusivity in service.

In the end, empathy is not just a skill—it is a mindset. It is about choosing to care, to understand, and to connect. When we lead with empathy, we elevate the service experience, creating moments that customers remember and appreciate. In a world where efficiency and speed often take precedence, businesses that embrace empathy set themselves apart.

Empathy is the heart of outstanding service. The more we practice it, the more we transform not only our interactions but also the entire experience for those we serve.

The Power of Validation

Validation is one of the most underrated yet powerful tools in service. It is the act of acknowledging and affirming a customer's feelings, experiences, and concerns. When customers feel validated, they feel seen, heard, and valued, which creates a lasting positive impression and strengthens their trust in a business.

At its core, validation is about making customers feel that their emotions and opinions matter. It doesn't mean agreeing with everything they say, but rather acknowledging their perspective in a way that makes them feel respected. Whether a customer is expressing frustration, excitement, or confusion, a validating response reassures them that they are important.

One of the most common scenarios where validation plays a key role is in handling complaints. Imagine a customer approaches you, upset about an incorrect order. A dismissive response like, "That's just how it is," or "There's nothing we can do," escalates their frustration. Instead, a validating response, such as "I understand how that could be frustrating. Let me see how I can fix this for you," immediately defuses tension and reassures the customer that their concern is taken seriously.

Validation also fosters deeper customer engagement. When a customer shares a positive experience, taking a moment to acknowledge it makes them feel appreciated. Saying something as simple as, "That's wonderful to hear! We love knowing that you enjoyed your visit," strengthens their connection to the business and increases the likelihood of them returning.

In fast-paced environments, it can be easy to overlook validation, but incorporating it into daily service interactions doesn't take much effort. Active listening plays a significant role in validation. Instead of just hearing what a customer is saying, take the time to truly listen, respond thoughtfully, and acknowledge their emotions.

This attitude/mindset is reflected in the use of phrases like the following:

- "I completely understand why that would be important to you."
- "That makes perfect sense."
- "I appreciate you sharing that with me."
- "You're absolutely right."
- "I can see how that would be frustrating."

These simple yet powerful statements reassure customers that they are not being brushed off. Validation also goes beyond words—it can be conveyed through body language. Nodding, maintaining eye contact, and mirroring a customer's tone and energy can reinforce that their emotions are being acknowledged. It is important to note that your tone can never rise in dealing with a complaint.

Businesses that prioritize validation create an environment of trust and loyalty. When customers feel understood, they are more likely to return, refer others, and become long-term advocates. Employees who practice validation also experience more positive interactions, reducing workplace stress and fostering a culture of mutual respect.

To cultivate validation in service, we must:

- Listen actively and acknowledge customers' emotions.
- Use affirming language to show understanding.
- Offer solutions while reinforcing the customer's perspective.
- Maintain positive body language to support verbal validation.
- Train teams to prioritize validation in their interactions.

Ultimately, validation is about making people feel valued. When customers feel like they matter, they return not just for a product or service but mainly and often only for the experience of being heard and respected. In a world where customers have endless options, businesses that embrace the power of validation set themselves apart and build lasting relationships based on trust and appreciation.

Accepting Blame When Dealing with an Upset Customer: A Delicate Art

When a customer is upset, the first instinct for many is to defend themselves or their company. However, this defensive reaction can often escalate the situation, deepening the customer's dissatisfaction. The ability to accept blame in a way that shows empathy and understanding, without admitting liability unless you are the owner, is a powerful tool for resolving conflicts and maintaining positive customer relationships. In this section, we'll explore how to navigate these tricky waters, balance empathy with professionalism, and understand the fine line between accepting blame and admitting liability.

The Importance of Accepting Blame

Why Accepting Blame Works

When a customer is upset, it's not always about the specifics of what went wrong; it is also about how they are made to feel. In many cases, customers feel unimportant, neglected, or ignored, which compounds their frustration. The feeling of not being listened to or understood can be just as damaging as the initial issue itself. By accepting blame, you demonstrate that you are taking the time to listen and acknowledge the customer's feelings. This does not mean you're admitting fault or taking responsibility for the company's errors but, rather, that you are validating the customer's experience.

The psychological impact of being acknowledged and having someone say, "I'm sorry that this happened," is enormous. It can defuse intense emotions and prevent the conversation from spiraling further. While this action may not resolve the issue immediately, it begins the process of diffusing tension and establishing a foundation for a solution. In this way, accepting blame serves as the first step in reestablishing trust between the business and the customer.

The Power of Empathy

Empathy plays a pivotal role in the art of accepting blame. Customers often just want to know that they are being heard, that their frustration is being understood. When an upset customer feels like they're being empathized with, it has the power to transform a negative experience into a positive one.

Empathy goes beyond simply offering an apology. It's about demonstrating that you can relate to how the customer is feeling. You might not be able to change what happened, but you can control how the customer feels in the moment. For example, a simple phrase like, "I understand how frustrating this must be for you," lets the customer know that you are not only aware of their issue but are also emotionally attuned to their experience.

When Not to Admit Liability

Liability Versus Blame

One of the most critical distinctions to make when dealing with upset customers is the difference between accepting blame and admitting liability. Accepting blame means acknowledging the issue or situation and showing empathy for the customer's experience, whereas admitting liability involves accepting legal responsibility for the problem.

As a frontline employee, your role is to manage the situation and help find a resolution without overstepping your boundaries. While it's crucial to accept blame when dealing with an upset customer, you should not, under any circumstances, admit liability unless you are the owner or are authorized to do so. Admitting liability prematurely can have severe consequences, both legally and financially, and can jeopardize your company's position.

Why You Shouldn't Admit Liability

Admitting liability can open the door to legal ramifications. When you admit that the business is at fault, it can be interpreted as an official admission, and, in some cases, it can lead to lawsuits or other legal actions. It's important to remember that liability is a legal term that has far-reaching consequences. A company is legally bound by the statements made by its employees, especially in cases where admissions are made outside of policy.

In many situations, the problem the customer is facing might not be entirely the company's fault. It could be a misunderstanding, an isolated incident, or an issue that falls outside of the scope of the employee's responsibility. By admitting liability, you're taking on responsibility for something you might not fully control or understand, and that's a dangerous precedent to set.

The Role of the Owner or Legal Representative

Only the owner or a person designated by the company should be the one to admit liability. In many cases, the owner or senior management has a clear understanding of the situation and the potential implications of taking legal responsibility. Employees, however, are typically not trained in legal matters and should avoid stepping into this territory unless explicitly directed to do so. It's important to follow the company's guidelines on when and how liability should be admitted.

Instead of admitting liability, focus on resolving the issue in a manner that benefits the customer while protecting the company's interests. Offer an apology, show empathy, and offer solutions that demonstrate the company's commitment to customer satisfaction.

How to Accept Blame Without Admitting Liability

Use Language That Accepts Responsibility Without Admitting Fault

One of the most effective ways to accept blame without admitting liability is by using language that shows responsibility for the situation while avoiding legal implications. The key is to focus on the customer's feelings and the situation, not necessarily the cause of the problem. For example:

- "I'm really sorry for the frustration this has caused you. I can understand why you're upset."
- "I apologize for this experience, and I'll do everything I can to make it right."
- "I'm sorry that this didn't meet your expectations. Let's find a solution together."

By using language like this, you're accepting blame for the customer's experience without admitting fault or liability. You're not claiming responsibility for the error; you're simply acknowledging that something went wrong and the customer's feelings are valid.

Focus on Solutions, Not the Problem

While acknowledging the issue is essential, focusing too much on the problem can prevent resolution. Once you've accepted blame and demonstrated empathy, shift the conversation to a solution. Customers want to feel like their concerns are being addressed and that the business is willing to go the extra mile to make things right.

Offer potential solutions and let the customer know what steps you'll take to ensure the issue doesn't happen again. For example:

- "I can offer you a replacement product or a refund if that's more convenient for you."
- "I will make sure to escalate this to management so we can address it and prevent this from happening again."

Offering solutions shows that you're not just listening to the problem but, in fact, you're actively working toward a resolution.

Document the Situation

To protect yourself and the business, always document the situation. Record the details of the incident, including what transpired, what was said, and any actions taken. This documentation can be helpful if the situation escalates or if management needs to follow up. It also ensures that you have a record of the customer's complaint and your response, which can be useful for future reference.

Dealing with Escalations

Know When to Escalate

In some cases, accepting blame and offering a solution may not be enough to calm an upset customer. If the customer continues to escalate, it may be time to bring in a manager or supervisor. This is especially important if the situation involves a potential legal matter or if the customer insists on blaming the company for something that is outside your control.

When escalating a situation, ensure that the customer knows they are being handed over to someone who can address the issue more effectively. For example:

- "I understand that you're upset, and I want to make sure this is resolved to your satisfaction. Let me get my manager to assist you."

Escalating the issue to a higher authority can demonstrate to the customer that their complaint is being taken seriously. It also removes you from the responsibility of resolving an issue that might be beyond your scope.

Accepting blame when dealing with an upset customer is an essential skill in customer service, but it's crucial to remember that accepting blame is not the same as admitting liability. While empathy and understanding are vital for calming down frustrated customers, admitting liability can have serious consequences for the company. As an employee, your role is to manage the situation, listen attentively, and offer solutions without overstepping boundaries. Always focus on the customer's experience and how you can make things right while protecting both your own interests and those of the company.

In the end, the art of accepting blame without admitting liability is about balancing empathy with professionalism, focusing on solutions, and ensuring that every customer interaction contributes to a positive experience—one that leaves them feeling heard, valued, and, most importantly, willing to return.

PART 3

Leadership and Service Culture

Leadership in service is not about authority but about influence—it's the ability to inspire others to deliver exceptional experiences by setting the example, fostering a sense of ownership, and creating a culture where service excellence becomes the standard, not the exception.

CHAPTER 9

Service Is an Experience: Passion, Ownership, and Energy

Passion Is Your Superpower: Love What You Do, Own What You Serve

There is a secret weapon in the service industry that sets the extraordinary apart from the ordinary. It is not just skill, experience, or knowledge—though those things certainly help. The most powerful force in delivering world-class service is passion. Passion for people. Passion for connection. Passion for creating an experience that customers will remember and return for.

Passion transforms a simple job into a calling. It fuels your energy, makes you stand out, and helps you connect with customers in a way that is authentic and magnetic. When you truly love what you do, it shows in everything—from the way you greet customers to the way you handle challenges. Customers can feel when someone is simply doing a job versus when someone genuinely cares. That energy is contagious, and it builds customer loyalty like nothing else.

How Passion Elevates Your Performance

1. **Passion Drives Excellence**

   When you love what you do, you naturally seek to do it better. You look for ways to improve, refine, and enhance the customer experience. Passionate people do not settle for "good enough." They aim for excellence in every interaction, creating an environment where both customers and colleagues thrive.

2. **Passion Creates Memorable Moments**

   Have you ever walked into a place and felt instantly welcome? That's not an accident. It happens because the person serving you is engaged, warm, and enthusiastic about their role. These moments stick with customers and keep them coming back.

3. **Passion Overcomes Challenges**

   In service, not every day is easy. There are difficult customers, unexpected problems, and days when things don't go as planned. But when you love what you do, you find ways to navigate challenges with grace. Passion helps you see problems as opportunities to create solutions and exceed expectations.

Cultivating Passion in Your Work

Some people may think, "What if I don't naturally feel passionate about service?" Passion is not always something that just appears; it can be cultivated. Here's how:

- **Find Your "Purpose"**—Why do you do what you do? Is it the joy of making someone's day? The challenge of delivering the best experience? The opportunity to brighten someone's mood? When you connect with your "why, your purpose," passion follows.
- **Master Your Craft**—The more confident and skilled you become, the more you'll enjoy your work. Invest in learning, practicing, and refining your service skills.
- **Surround Yourself with Passionate People**—Energy is contagious. Work with, learn from, and be inspired by those who love what they do.
- **Create Personal Connections**—The more you engage with customers, the more rewarding your job becomes. Each person you serve is an opportunity to create a positive impact.

Owning What You Serve

Service is not just about delivering a product or transaction; it's about delivering an experience. When you take ownership of your role, you elevate not only your own performance but also the perception of the brand you represent.

- **Take Pride in Your Role**—No matter what position you hold, whether as a barista, server, frontline customer representative, or manager, your role is crucial. Own it, and be the best at it.
- **Be Fully Present**—Customers notice when someone is truly engaged versus when they are just going through the motions. Give them your full attention.
- **Be Proactive**—Anticipate customer needs before they even ask. This level of care sets the best apart from the rest.

Passion Is the Difference

Passion is what makes the best service experiences unforgettable. It is the energy that turns customers into loyal fans. When you love what you do, it doesn't just benefit your workplace—it benefits you. You enjoy your job more, you create deeper connections, and you feel fulfilled knowing that you are making a difference, one customer at a time.

So, embrace your passion. Love what you do. Own what you serve. And watch how it transforms everything.

You Are the Face of the Business

In every customer-facing role, there is one undeniable truth: **You are the face of the business**. The moment you step into your workplace, your actions, words, and demeanor shape how customers perceive the company. Whether you're in hospitality, retail, health care, or any other service industry, the experience you provide leaves a lasting impression. Customers may forget what they ordered, but they will never forget how you made them feel.

First Impressions Set the Tone

Within the first 15 seconds of an interaction, a customer has already formed an opinion about you and the business. Your body language, facial expressions, and tone of voice, all contribute to this initial impression. A warm smile, confident posture, and enthusiastic greeting can immediately create a welcoming environment.

More than price or product, what truly drives customers away is feeling invisible, overlooked, or dismissed by the very people they trust to serve them. David Bater reminds us that 68 percent of customers leave not because of what's on offer, but because they sense a lack of care. That first interaction is a crossroads; it shapes how they feel, what they remember, and whether they come back. When we show genuine attention and respect, we don't just earn business—we build lasting relationships rooted in trust and human connection.

Key Takeaway: Always start with positivity. A friendly "Good morning! How are you today?" instantly makes customers feel valued and appreciated.

Your Energy Is Contagious

Customers feed off the energy you bring to an interaction. If you're enthusiastic, they feel excited. If you're indifferent, they notice. Your tone, engagement, and willingness to help create the atmosphere of the entire business.

- Speak with warmth and sincerity.
- Show genuine interest in the customer's needs.
- Reflect excitement and passion for what you do.

Customers return to businesses they trust. Trust is built through consistency, reliability, and authenticity. If you provide great service once, they may be pleased. If you do it every time, they become loyal.

- Follow through on promises.
- Show knowledge and confidence in the product or service.
- Take ownership of problems and find solutions quickly.

Example: Imagine a customer has a minor issue with their order. Instead of dismissing their concern, you acknowledge it, apologize, and correct it promptly. That simple act of service can turn a frustrated customer into a lifelong supporter.

Mastering Positive Language

The words you choose shape the customer's experience. Positive, solution-focused language fosters a sense of care and attentiveness.

Instead of:

- "I don't know." → Say: "Let me find out for you."
- "That's not my department." → Say: "I'll connect you with the right person."
- "We're out of that." → Say: "That item is currently unavailable, but I'd love to recommend something similar."

The Power of Small Gestures

Customers remember the little things:

- A genuine compliment
- Remembering their name
- A personal touch, like asking about their day
- A thank-you as they leave.

These small gestures create an emotional connection, making customers feel valued beyond just the transaction.

Your Role Extends Beyond the Counter

Whether you're an employee, a manager, or an owner, **you set the standard for service excellence**. Your example influences colleagues and shapes the workplace culture. Leading by example with enthusiasm, professionalism, and a customer-first mindset inspires those around you to do the same.

Every interaction is an opportunity to create a positive experience. Your actions define the business in the eyes of every customer you serve.

Be intentional, be present, and, most importantly, be the person who makes customers return—not because they have to but because they want to.

You are not just an employee—you are the business. Make every moment count.

CHAPTER 10

Internal Customer Service: The Role of Teamwork and Leadership

Team Service: The Role of Internal Customer Service

Service isn't just about customers—it's also about how teams serve each other. Internal customer service refers to the way employees interact and support one another within the workplace. When team members work together cohesively, service quality improves across the board.

Supporting One Another

A well-functioning team shares responsibilities and looks out for one another. This includes:

Communicating clearly and effectively.
Stepping in to assist during busy periods.
Acknowledging and appreciating each other's efforts.

The Ripple Effect of Internal Service

When employees treat one another with respect and professionalism, this culture extends to customer interactions. A positive work environment fosters enthusiasm, which customers can sense and appreciate. When you nail team spirit, the result is electric in service, and the atmosphere is perfect.

Creating a Culture of Mutual Respect

Encouraging team service involves:

- Providing constructive feedback
- Celebrating team achievements
- Practicing active listening with colleagues

By fostering a strong internal service culture, businesses ensure that both employees and customers receive exceptional treatment, leading to better overall performance and customer satisfaction.

Why Service Is So Important

Service is the foundation of any successful business. It is the bridge between a company and its customers, shaping reputations, building loyalty, and driving growth. Without exceptional service, even the best products or most competitive prices can fall short. Below, we explore why service is so critical and how it influences every aspect of business and human interaction.

1. **Service Builds Loyalty**

   Great service creates loyal customers who return time and time again. Loyalty is not just about convenience or pricing; it is built on trust and positive experiences. Customers who feel valued and appreciated are more likely to choose a business repeatedly, even if competitors offer similar or better deals. Loyalty leads to long-term customer relationships and turns one-time buyers into lifelong patrons.

2. **Service Differentiates You from Competitors**

   In a world where products and services can be easily replicated, customer service is often the defining factor that sets a business apart. Many companies sell similar items, but the way they treat their customers makes the difference. Whether it is through personalized interactions, prompt problem-solving, or a genuine commitment to customer satisfaction, service becomes a key competitive advantage.

3. **Service Creates Positive Word-of-Mouth Marketing**

   Customers who experience outstanding service are more likely to share their experiences with friends, family, and colleagues. Positive word-of-mouth marketing is one of the most powerful tools a business can have because people trust recommendations from those they know. When service is extraordinary, customers naturally become brand ambassadors, spreading the word about their great experiences.

4. **Service Impacts Customer Satisfaction**

   Customer satisfaction goes beyond just meeting expectations—it is about exceeding them. When customers feel heard, understood, and cared for, they leave interactions feeling satisfied. Satisfied customers not only return but also contribute to a positive brand image and overall company success.

5. **Service Increases Revenue and Growth**

   Studies consistently show that businesses that prioritize service tend to generate higher revenues. Customers are willing to spend more when they receive excellent service. Moreover, satisfied customers are more likely to make repeat purchases and explore additional offerings from the business. This directly translates to increased sales and sustainable growth.

6. **Service Fosters a Positive Work Culture**

   Excellent service does not just benefit customers—it also creates a positive work environment for employees. When businesses emphasize service, employees develop a sense of pride in their work. A customer-focused culture fosters teamwork, motivation, and job satisfaction. Happy employees, in turn, provide better service, creating a cycle of positivity and excellence.

7. **Service Enhances Brand Reputation**

   A company's reputation is built on how it treats its customers. In today's digital age, where reviews and ratings can make or break a business, exceptional service is more important than ever. A strong reputation for service attracts new customers and reassures existing ones that they are in good hands.

8. **Service Helps in Crisis Management**

   Every business faces challenges, from product defects to logistical issues. When problems arise, service plays a crucial role in damage control. A well-trained service team can turn a negative situation into a positive one by handling complaints professionally, offering solutions, and demonstrating genuine care for customer concerns. How a business responds in difficult moments often determines customer retention and long-term success.

9. **Service Is an Opportunity to Make a Difference**

   Beyond business growth, great service has a human element—it has the power to brighten someone's day. A kind word, a helpful gesture, or simply taking the time to listen can leave a lasting impact on a customer's experience. Service is an opportunity to connect, uplift, and make a real difference in people's lives.

   Service is more than a business function—it is an experience, a philosophy, and a commitment to excellence. It is the defining factor that influences customer loyalty, differentiates businesses, fosters positive relationships, and drives long-term success. Every touchpoint, every interaction, and every engagement is an opportunity to create a meaningful experience. When businesses and individuals prioritize service, they unlock the true potential of their relationships, their reputation, and their future.

Everyone Is on the Same Team: Building Unity and Cooperation

In any successful business, the ultimate goal is to provide exceptional service that exceeds customer expectations, builds loyalty, and drives growth. However, achieving this goal requires more than just individual effort; it demands a unified, collective approach where every member of the team is working together toward a common purpose. **When everyone understands that they are on the same team**, not only will the service experience improve, but the internal culture will also thrive, making the workplace more enjoyable, efficient, and productive. In any thriving business, delivering outstanding service that delights customers, fosters loyalty, and supports growth isn't just an individual goal—it's a shared mission that thrives on teamwork. When everyone is aligned and working toward a common objective, the result is a more positive, productive, and enjoyable workplace.

As leadership expert Patrick Lencioni famously stated, *"If you could get all the people in an organization rowing in the same direction, you could dominate any industry, in any market, against any competition, at any time"* (Lencioni 2002). This quote underscores the power of alignment and unity across a team—when everyone is truly working together, anything is possible.

Whether you're managing a small café, a large corporate office, or any other customer-facing industry, this principle applies universally: **We rise by lifting each other**.

Collaboration Drives Success

The phrase "teamwork makes the dream work" may sound cliché, but its truth cannot be overstated. In any business, when each person understands and embraces their role, the collective effort leads to a smoother, more efficient operation. This collaboration directly impacts customer satisfaction and service quality.

Imagine walking into a café where the barista greets you with a warm smile, the server promptly offers you a menu, and the cook prepares your meal with precision. Behind this seamless experience, there's a team working together to ensure that every step of the process runs smoothly. The barista knows their job inside out, but they don't just focus on making coffee—they're part of a greater system that includes servers, cooks, and managers, all of whom rely on each other's contributions to provide a cohesive experience.

When each team member sees the bigger picture and understands that their work impacts others, the entire team functions more effectively, which results in happier customers and better business outcomes.

A team that operates in harmony can provide customers with a seamless and memorable experience. A breakdown in communication or a lack of cooperation can create frustrations that customers easily pick up on. For example, if a server forgets to communicate an order modification to the kitchen, it can result in an unhappy customer who feels neglected. However, when everyone is on the same page and works together, the experience is smooth, efficient, and positive for the customer.

Customers don't just judge the quality of the product; they judge the entire experience, from the moment they walk in the door to when they leave. When employees work in unison, this synergy is palpable to the customer, fostering trust and encouraging loyalty. A positive experience leads to word-of-mouth referrals, repeat business, and a stronger brand reputation.

Leaders Set the Tone

A successful team is built on strong leadership. Leaders aren't just task managers; they are culture creators. The most effective leaders create environments where teamwork is not just encouraged but also celebrated. When a leader demonstrates respect for each team member's role, communicates openly, and fosters a sense of shared responsibility, they set the tone for the rest of the team.

Modeling Behavior

Great leaders lead by example. If a leader shows respect for their team and is committed to doing their part, the team will follow suit. For instance, if the leader takes time to support a team member in need, help with tasks, or step in when things get hectic, the message is clear: No job is beneath anyone, and no one is too important to pitch in. This builds mutual respect and strengthens the sense of **shared purpose**.

Leaders should also encourage transparency and open communication. When team members are comfortable expressing their thoughts, ideas, and concerns without fear of judgment, they are more likely to collaborate and solve problems together. This approach not only enhances performance but also fosters trust, creating a workplace where people feel heard and valued.

Effective communication is the cornerstone of any successful team. Leaders must prioritize open, honest, and respectful communication at all levels. This means not only providing clear expectations but also listening to feedback and encouraging dialogue between team members.

When communication flows freely and effectively, misunderstandings and mistakes are less likely to occur. Team members are more likely to support one another, share information, and work collaboratively to solve problems. Whether it's during daily check-ins, team meetings, or casual conversations, keeping communication lines open builds stronger bonds among employees and reinforces the idea that everyone is in it together.

Respecting Everyone's Role

Every team member, regardless of their position, plays an integral role in the overall success of the business. It's important to remember that the janitor, the kitchen team, the frontline servers, the managers, and the secretary, all contribute to creating an environment where customers feel welcomed and well-cared-for. No task is too small, and every role is significant.

When everyone on the team feels respected, they are more likely to give their best effort and go above and beyond for customers. Encouraging mutual respect creates a positive work environment where each person feels like a valued part of the team. For instance, a server who appreciates the effort of the kitchen staff is more likely to communicate effectively and avoid unnecessary delays, while the kitchen staff is motivated to prepare high-quality meals for customers.

Recognition is one of the most powerful tools in building a cohesive team. It's easy to overlook the day-to-day contributions of employees, but when leaders and team members take the time to acknowledge each other's efforts, it reinforces the idea that everyone's hard work is essential to the business's success.

Celebrating both small and large achievements builds morale and reinforces the notion that the team is working toward shared goals. Recognition could be as simple as verbally thanking someone for their contribution, holding regular team celebrations, or even offering formal awards for outstanding service. The act of celebrating achievements, no matter how big or small, creates a sense of pride and unity.

Collaboration over Competition

In a team-oriented environment, collaboration should always take precedence over competition. When employees feel pitted against one another, it can lead to tension, miscommunication, and a lack of cohesion. Instead, businesses should foster an atmosphere where cooperation is the norm.

Encouraging teamwork means emphasizing the collective success of the team over individual achievement. Leaders should create opportunities for team members to collaborate, problem-solve together, and share their expertise. This collaborative environment ensures that employees feel supported and that no one is left to struggle alone.

Creating Shared Goals

Setting shared goals for the team helps everyone align with the business's objectives. These goals should be clear, measurable, and achievable and should focus on both the quality of the customer experience and the internal workings of the business. When team members understand the broader objectives, they can work toward them more effectively, knowing that their success contributes to the success of the entire team.

For example, setting goals such as improving customer satisfaction scores or reducing response times to customer complaints can help the team work together toward common benchmarks. As each team member sees their individual efforts contributing to these collective goals, they will feel more connected and motivated to give their best.

Overcoming Challenges as a Unified Team

Handling Conflict Constructively

Even the best teams encounter conflicts, whether it's a difference of opinion, personality clash, or disagreement over how things should be done. However, how conflicts are handled can make all the difference in maintaining a positive and productive environment.

The key is to approach conflict with a mindset of problem-solving rather than blame. Encourage employees to address conflicts respectfully and work together to find solutions. By modeling constructive conflict resolution, leaders can help ensure that disagreements don't tear the team apart but rather lead to stronger collaboration.

Learning from Mistakes Together

Mistakes are inevitable, but how a team responds to them is what sets successful businesses apart. Instead of pointing fingers or assigning blame, a strong team should view mistakes as learning opportunities. Discuss what went wrong, what can be done differently next time, and how the team can collectively prevent similar issues from arising in the future. When employees know that they won't be penalized for mistakes but will be supported in learning from them, they are more likely to take ownership of their actions and work toward improvement.

Unity Drives Success

In any business, creating a culture where **everyone is on the same team** is essential for long-term success. When leaders foster collaboration, communication, and respect, they set the foundation for a team that works in unison to provide exceptional customer experiences. Teamwork is not just about getting the job done—it's about building a culture of trust, mutual support, and shared purpose that drives growth, both internally and externally.

By embracing the principle that everyone is on the same team, businesses can cultivate an environment where employees feel valued, supported, and motivated to give their best. This, in turn, leads to happier customers, stronger relationships, and greater success. The strength of your team is the foundation of your business's success, and when everyone pulls together, the possibilities are endless.

CHAPTER 11

AI, Chatbots, and the Future of Service: Balancing Tech and the Human Touch

AI, Chatbots, and the Human Touch: The Future of Service

The way customers interact with businesses has changed dramatically. Instead of visiting physical stores or calling customer service lines, most interactions now happen through apps and self-service portals. While technology has made service faster and more efficient, it has also created a challenge: How do businesses build genuine emotional connections when human interaction is minimized?

Emotional intelligence isn't just about reading facial expressions or hearing tone of voice—it's about understanding needs, frustrations, and expectations. Even in a digital-first world, customers still want to feel valued, understood, and heard. The brands that succeed in this environment will be those that bring emotional intelligence into their digital experiences.

Businesses are embracing automation **to cut costs, speed up service, and stay ahead of the competition.** But in this rush toward efficiency, one question remains: **Can AI ever replace human connection?**

It's easy to see why companies are investing in AI. A chatbot can answer thousands of queries in seconds. Automated systems don't take breaks, call in sick, or have off days. AI never forgets a detail, never gets frustrated, and never needs a pay rise. On paper, it sounds perfect. But service isn't just about answering questions or processing transactions—it's about people. It's about making **customers feel seen, heard, and valued.** And that's where technology alone falls short.

Think about the last time you needed help and got stuck in an automated loop, desperately pressing buttons to reach a human. Or the moment you asked a chatbot for something specific, only to receive generic responses that didn't actually solve your problem. AI can handle the basics, but it lacks intuition. It doesn't recognize frustration in a customer's voice; nor can it offer empathy in a difficult moment. It does not have the emotional intelligence needed to truly connect. These are the things that turn good service into unforgettable service.

Businesses need to find a balance. **AI and automation aren't the enemy; they're just tools.** Used well, they can enhance service, making it smoother and more efficient. But the best businesses know that technology should support human connection, not replace it. Customers don't just want fast answers; they want to feel understood. They don't just remember what you did for them; they remember how you made them feel.

Throughout this part of the book, we'll explore how businesses can use AI without losing the human touch. We'll look at real-world examples of companies that get it right—and those that don't. We'll dive into strategies that allow technology to work alongside people, ensuring that service remains personal, engaging, and, most importantly, exceptional.

The future of service isn't about choosing between AI and human connection—it's about knowing when to use each to create an experience customers won't forget.

How AI and Chatbots Became Essential in Customer Service

AI and chatbots have transformed customer service, reshaping the way businesses interact with their customers. From simple automated responses to sophisticated AI-driven solutions, technology has come a long way in bridging the gap between efficiency and engagement. But how did we get here?

The journey of AI in customer service began with basic automated phone systems in the 1980s. Interactive Voice Response (IVR) allowed companies to route calls without a human operator, setting the stage for automation in service. As the Internet grew, e-mail support became common, followed by live chat options in the early 2000s. However, the real shift happened with the rise of machine learning (ML) and natural language processing (NLP), enabling AI to understand and respond to customer inquiries more effectively.

Today, AI-driven chatbots handle millions of customer interactions daily. Businesses leverage AI not just for cost-cutting but also to provide faster, round-the-clock assistance. The appeal is clear: AI never tires, works 24/7, and can process inquiries at an unmatched speed. **But does this efficiency come at a cost to the customer experience?**

Where AI Works Best

AI excels in areas where speed, consistency, and scalability are critical. Some key advantages include:

- **Speed and Efficiency**—AI-driven chatbots can resolve basic inquiries instantly, reducing wait times for customers.
- **24/7 Availability**—Unlike human agents, AI doesn't need breaks or sleep, ensuring customers receive support at any time.
- **Consistency**—AI provides standardized responses, ensuring brand messaging remains uniform across all interactions.
- **Multilingual Support**—AI tools can translate and respond in multiple languages, eliminating language barriers.
- **Data Analysis and Personalization**—AI tracks customer interactions, learning from past engagements to offer tailored recommendations and solutions.

Many businesses have found success in integrating AI into their service models.

Case Studies: Companies Excelling in AI-Driven Service

1. **Amazon's Alexa**—Amazon has seamlessly integrated AI into customer interactions with Alexa, offering voice-activated support, product recommendations, and order tracking. Alexa's ability to understand and respond to customer needs has set a high standard for AI in service.
2. **Sephora's Chatbot**—Beauty retailer Sephora uses AI-driven chatbots to assist customers with product recommendations, virtual

makeup try-ons, and appointment scheduling. This has enhanced customer engagement while freeing human employees to **focus on in-store experiences.**

3. **Apple's Siri**—Siri has revolutionized voice-activated customer assistance, allowing users to find information, set reminders, give definitions, mark your parked car, and troubleshoot problems without human intervention. Apple's continuous improvements in voice AI have made Siri a valuable support tool.

These companies demonstrate that AI, when used strategically, can enhance customer service by making interactions more seamless and efficient. However, **AI isn't a perfect solution.**

Where AI Struggles

Despite its many strengths, AI has limitations that prevent it from fully replacing human service. Some key challenges include:

- **Lack of Emotional Intelligence**—AI cannot read subtle emotions or provide genuine empathy, which is crucial in sensitive customer interactions.
- **Handling Complex Issues**—AI struggles with multistep problems that require human judgment and flexibility.
- **Frustration with Generic Responses**—Customers often become frustrated when AI fails to provide personalized or relevant solutions.
- **Overreliance on Automation**—Businesses that depend too much on AI risk alienating customers who prefer human interaction.

The Balancing Act

AI is a powerful tool, but it is not a **replacement for human connection.** The best businesses use AI to enhance service while ensuring that customers still have access to real people when needed. The future of customer service isn't AI versus human—it's a blend of both, creating an experience that is **efficient yet personal,** automated yet warm.

The Danger of Losing the Personal Touch

AI is excellent at handling routine tasks, providing fast and efficient responses, and automating repetitive interactions. But when businesses rely too heavily on AI, service can become cold, impersonal, and purely transactional. Instead of fostering connections, AI risks turning customer interactions into mechanical exchanges that lack warmth, empathy, and human understanding.

A truly great service experience is more than just solving a problem—it's about how customers feel during and after the interaction. The moment service becomes purely transactional, businesses start losing what makes them memorable.

The Dehumanization of Service

When service loses its human element, customer relationships suffer. AI-driven customer interactions, if not carefully designed, can feel robotic. Automated responses, rigid decision trees, and a lack of emotional intelligence can lead to frustrating experiences, pushing customers away rather than drawing them in.

Consider the difference between:

- A chatbot that provides a generic apology when a problem arises.
- A human service rep who listens, expresses genuine concern, and goes the extra mile to fix the issue.

Customers remember how a business made them feel, not just what it did for them. Removing the human touch can turn once-loyal customers into frustrated, one-time buyers.

AI Can't Replace Genuine Human Connection

Some service experiences thrive on personalization and human warmth—areas where AI still struggles. Imagine walking into a café where the barista remembers your name and favorite drink. Or visiting a clothing store where an associate gives expert advice tailored to your style. AI can provide recommendations, but it lacks the human intuition and emotional intelligence that make these experiences special.

The Airline Industry

The airline industry provides a clear example of the risks of transactional service. Automated check-ins and self-service kiosks have made air travel more efficient, but what happens when something goes wrong?

- **Automated Check-Ins:** Most airlines now use AI-powered kiosks and apps for check-ins, seat selections, and even boarding passes. This speeds up the process and reduces staffing needs.
- **Flight Cancellations:** When flights are delayed or cancelled, automation often falls short. AI may rebook a flight or provide a refund option, but it can't offer the reassurance and flexibility of a human agent who understands the stress and urgency of a disrupted travel plan.

Passengers facing cancellations often want more than a text notification—they want solutions, empathy, and support. Airlines that balance AI efficiency with human service ensure that when automation isn't enough, real people are there to step in.

The Best Service Experiences Blend AI with Emotional Intelligence

The future of service isn't about replacing people with AI—it's about enhancing human service with AI's capabilities. The most successful businesses recognize that while AI can handle routine tasks, human connection remains irreplaceable.

Augment, Don't Replace

AI should free up humans to focus on relationships, not remove them entirely. Businesses that use AI effectively allow their employees to spend less time on repetitive tasks and more time building real connections with customers.

The Ritz-Carlton Approach

The Ritz-Carlton is known for world-class hospitality, and while they leverage AI for efficiency, they never compromise on personal service.

- **AI in Efficiency:** The hotel chain uses AI to track guest preferences, anticipate needs, and streamline check-in and room service requests.
- **Humans at the Core:** Despite AI's role in operational efficiency, The Ritz-Carlton ensures that guest interactions remain warm, personal, and led by people, not machines.

Design AI Interactions with Warmth and Personalization

If AI must be part of the service experience, it should be designed with human-centric principles in mind:

- **Use Conversational AI:** Avoid robotic scripts—program AI to respond in natural, engaging ways.
- **Offer a Seamless Human Handoff:** Ensure customers can easily transition from AI to a human representative when needed.
- **Recognize Emotional Cues:** AI should detect frustration or confusion and escalate complex issues to real people.

Personalization in the Age of AI

AI doesn't have to replace human interactions—it can make them even better. By analyzing customer behavior, preferences, and past interactions, AI can provide hyper-personalized experiences that feel both seamless and intuitive.

Predictive Service: Anticipating Customer Needs

Companies like Spotify, Netflix, and leading e-commerce platforms use AI to predict what customers want before they even ask.

- **Spotify and Netflix:** AI analyzes listening and viewing habits to suggest music and shows tailored to user preferences.

- **E-commerce:** AI tracks past purchases and browsing behavior to recommend relevant products, increasing conversion rates.

Training AI to Recognize Human Emotions

For AI to support—not replace—human service, businesses must train it to detect emotional cues:

- **Frustration Detection:** If a chatbot senses frustration in a customer's tone or repeated interactions, it should escalate the issue to a human.
- **Empathy-Driven Responses:** AI can be programmed to recognize words that indicate distress and respond in ways that acknowledge emotion before offering solutions.

Sephora's AI-Powered Personalization

Sephora has embraced AI in both online and in-store experiences:

- **Virtual Try-On:** AI allows customers to test makeup products digitally before purchasing.
- **In-Store Experts:** Despite AI's convenience, Sephora still invests in knowledgeable in-store beauty advisers who offer personalized recommendations based on skin type, preferences, and trends.

The Key to Success: AI as an Enhancement, Not a Replacement

The businesses that thrive in the AI era will be those that use **technology to strengthen—not replace—human relationships**. AI can provide data-driven personalization, but it's the human touch that turns an ordinary service experience into an extraordinary one.

The Growing Resistance to AI-Driven Service

While many businesses are embracing AI to enhance efficiency and reduce costs, a growing segment of consumers is pushing back. These individuals refuse to support companies that replace human interaction with automation, arguing that AI-driven service strips away the warmth, empathy, and personal connection that make customer experiences meaningful. It does not want to see human jobs replaced.

This movement isn't just about preference—it's about values. Many consumers see the shift toward automation as a broader societal issue, believing that if businesses prioritize AI over human relationships, society will suffer as a whole.

Why Some Consumers Reject AI in Service

1. **The Loss of Human Connection**

   For many, service is about more than just getting a product or answer—it's about feeling valued. AI, no matter how advanced, lacks genuine emotion. Customers who value eye contact, real conversations, and spontaneous interactions often feel disconnected when AI takes center stage.

2. **Ethical Concerns**

   There's a moral aspect to this resistance. Some individuals see AI replacing human jobs as a negative societal shift. They worry about:
   - The loss of employment opportunities for service workers.
   - The erosion of meaningful customer service careers.
   - The long-term consequences of replacing people with machines.

3. **Frustration with AI's Limitations**

   Even those who appreciate technology often find AI frustrating in customer service. Automated responses, chatbots that fail to understand complex requests, and self-checkout systems that malfunction contribute to the growing sentiment that AI is not always an improvement.

The Rise of AI-Free Businesses

In response to this movement, some companies are choosing to market themselves as "AI-free" or "human-first" businesses. These brands emphasize:

- **Human customer service teams instead of chatbots**
- **Personalized, face-to-face interactions**
- **A commitment to keeping jobs in customer service sectors**

Examples include small, independent bookstores, boutique hotels, and specialty coffee shops that proudly promote their human-centered approach as a key selling point.

The Hospitality Industry's Diverging Paths

The hospitality sector illustrates the divide between AI adoption and consumer pushback.

- **AI-Driven Hotels:** Some hotels now offer fully automated check-in, AI-powered concierge services, and robot room service. While efficient, these innovations can feel impersonal.
- **Human-Centric Hotels:** In contrast, high-end hospitality brands like boutique hotels highlight their commitment to personalized guest experiences, ensuring human staff handle guest needs with care and authenticity.

The Future: Will Businesses Listen to AI-Resistant Consumers?

As AI continues to evolve, businesses will have to decide whether to lean fully into automation or maintain a balance that caters to consumers who value human connection. Companies that ignore this growing resistance risk alienating customers who want more than just efficiency—they want to feel seen, heard, and valued.

The challenge for businesses is clear: Can they harness AI without sacrificing the human touch? Those who strike the right balance will be the ones who thrive in this evolving landscape.

The Shift to @Table Ordering

Restaurants and cafés around the world are rapidly adopting @table ordering technology. By allowing customers to browse menus, place orders, and pay directly from their smartphones, businesses are streamlining service, increasing table turnover, and—perhaps most importantly—boosting average spend. Studies have shown that when customers order through a digital interface, they are more likely to add extra items, upgrades, and impulse purchases without the pressure of a traditional server interaction.

For businesses, the benefits are clear:

- **Higher Average Spend**—Customers tend to add more to their orders when using digital menus, especially with upsell prompts and suggested add-ons.
- **Faster Service and Efficiency**—Orders go straight to the kitchen, reducing wait times and improving workflow.
- **Reduced Labor Costs**—Fewer servers are needed, allowing businesses to optimize staffing levels and meet labor targets.
- **Customer Convenience**—Guests appreciate being able to order at their own pace without waiting for a server.

The Risk of Losing the Human Moment

While @table ordering makes service faster and more efficient, it also eliminates the human touchpoints that define great hospitality. Without face-to-face interaction, businesses risk losing:

- **Personalized Recommendations**—A skilled server doesn't just take orders; they guide the experience, suggesting pairings, specials, and dishes tailored to customer preferences.
- **Emotional Connection**—A warm greeting, a genuine smile, and a personal conversation turn a meal into an experience.
- **Problem Resolution**—When issues arise, human servers can read the situation, offer solutions, and ensure customer satisfaction in a way that AI cannot.

Restaurants Finding the Balance

Some businesses have embraced @table ordering as the new standard, while others are using it selectively to enhance—not replace—human interaction.

- **Full Automation:** Some quick-service restaurants and casual dining chains have moved entirely to @table ordering, reducing the need for servers and prioritizing speed and efficiency.

- **Hybrid Approach:** Many higher-end restaurants integrate @table ordering for convenience while ensuring that key service moments remain human-led. Servers are still present to greet guests, offer recommendations, and elevate the experience beyond what technology can provide.

Making Human Service Moments Powerful

If a restaurant adopts @table ordering, the moments where human service does occur need to be impactful. Businesses that thrive in this new model ensure that:

- **First Impressions Matter**—Staff welcome guests warmly, setting the tone for the experience before technology takes over.
- **Engagement Still Exists**—Even if ordering happens via a device, servers check in with customers, offering suggestions and ensuring satisfaction.
- **The Farewell Is Memorable**—A great goodbye leaves a lasting impression, ensuring customers feel valued beyond the transaction.

The Future of @Table Ordering: Finding the Right Mix

While @table ordering is here to stay, the most successful hospitality businesses will find ways to integrate it without losing the essence of great service. The restaurants that strike the right balance—leveraging technology while preserving human connection—will be the ones that customers return to time and time again.

The Key to Seamless AI and Human Integration

The best service experiences don't happen by accident—they are carefully designed to balance **efficiency with genuine human connection.** While AI can optimize workflows, answer routine questions, and handle repetitive tasks, it cannot replace the warmth, intuition, and adaptability of human service.

Achieving harmony between AI and human connection requires a strategic approach that enhances—not diminishes—the personal elements of customer interactions. The businesses that succeed will be those that recognize AI as a tool to support service professionals rather than as a substitute for them.

The Core Principles of AI-Enhanced Service

1. **AI as an Enabler, Not a Replacement**
   AI should free up human employees to focus on meaningful interactions rather than replace them entirely. Businesses must ensure that AI handles efficiency-driven tasks while service teams engage in personal, high-value interactions.

2. **Design AI with Empathy in Mind**
   AI-driven customer experiences should not feel robotic. By incorporating NLP, sentiment analysis, and personalized responses, businesses can make AI feel less transactional and more conversational.

3. **Seamless Human Handoffs**
   The transition from AI to human support should be frictionless. If AI cannot resolve an issue, it should immediately escalate to a knowledgeable service representative who can take over without making the customer repeat themselves.

4. **Humanizing Digital Interactions**
   Even AI-driven customer interactions should feel personal. Using names, remembering past preferences, and tailoring recommendations can create a more engaging experience.

5. **Empowering Employees to Work Alongside AI**
   The team should view AI as a collaborative tool that enhances their roles rather than replaces them. Training employees to use AI-driven insights can help them deliver even better service.

AI Isn't Going Anywhere—Yet Human Connection Is Irreplaceable

The rise of AI in customer service is inevitable. Businesses are investing in automation to improve efficiency, reduce costs, and provide

24/7 support. However, the companies that will truly thrive are the ones that recognize AI's role as a **support system for human service, not a replacement for it.**

Moving Beyond Cost-Cutting: AI as a Relationship Builder

Many businesses have historically implemented AI as a way to cut labor costs and streamline operations. While efficiency is important, service-driven businesses must **shift their mindset** from cost-cutting to relationship-building. AI should enhance the customer journey, making interactions smoother, more personalized, and more valuable—not just cheaper.

Technology should always serve people—not the other way around. Because at the heart of every great service experience is a simple truth: **Human connection is irreplaceable.**

The Businesses That Will Win Are the Ones That Master Both

It's not about choosing between automation and personal service—it's about seamlessly integrating the two.

Because here's the truth:

Loyalty isn't built on efficiency. It's built on how you make people feel.

The companies that get this right will lead the future of business. The ones that don't? They'll fade into the background because no one remembers soulless transactions.

So, how do you create personalized human service in an automated world?

1. **Make Technology Feel Human**

   Just because a system is automated doesn't mean it has to feel robotic. Language matters.

   Imagine you're ordering from an online store or scanning a QR code at a restaurant. You complete the process, and the screen simply says:

   "Order confirmed."

   That's it. No warmth. No engagement. No feeling.

Now imagine instead:

"Thanks for your order, [Name]! We can't wait for you to enjoy it. Let us know if there's anything we can do to make it perfect."

Same automation. An entirely different experience.

Key Takeaway: Use language that makes people feel like they're interacting with a brand that cares, not just a system that processes.

2. **Personalization at Scale**

   The biggest advantage of technology is the ability to personalize at scale.

   ○ Use customer names in order confirmations and follow-ups.

   ○ Send personalized recommendations based on past purchases.

   ○ Acknowledge special occasions—birthdays, anniversaries, milestones.

   Ever received a cold, generic marketing e-mail that had nothing to do with you? It probably landed in the trash. Now think about the times when a business actually remembered you—sent you a birthday discount or recommended something you genuinely needed. That's the difference.

   People don't want to feel like just another number in a database. They want to feel seen.

3. **Train for Human Moments**

   Even if tech handles transactions, humans create loyalty.

   Think about this:

   ○ A customer places an online order and instantly gets a personalized thank-you e-mail from the team.

   ○ A coffee shop remembers a regular's order and has it ready before they even ask.

   ○ A restaurant server steps in to recommend a dish based on past orders—even though the customer used a QR code to order.

   These moments of human connection turn first-time visitors into lifelong customers.

   Automation should enhance connection, not replace it.

4. **The Power of Surprise and Delight**

   People expect automation. What they don't expect are thoughtful, personal touches.

   ○ A handwritten note inside a delivered package

- A follow-up e-mail from a real person asking about their experience
- A small, unexpected upgrade because they've been a loyal customer
Tiny gestures. Huge impact.

5. **Empower Employees to Personalize the Experience**

No matter how advanced technology becomes, your people are your greatest asset.

The best businesses permit employees to create memorable experiences.

- A hotel front desk agent who upgrades a room for a returning guest
- A retail employee who offers a discount to a customer having a bad day
- A call center agent who sends a thank-you e-mail
These small moments create a massive emotional impact.

Technology Is Here to Stay—But So Is the Need for Hospitality

Automation isn't going anywhere. But the businesses that thrive will be the ones that understand this simple truth:

Efficiency gets customers in the door.
Connection keeps them coming back.

The world is becoming faster, more digital, and more automated. But human connection? That will always be the difference between a business that gets customers and a business that keeps them.

Your Challenge: How Will You Bring More Humanity into Automation?

Where can you infuse personal touchpoints into your customer journey? How can you make people feel valued—even in a digital world?

The businesses that figure this out will be the ones customers never forget.

Will yours be one of them?

Technology Should Serve People, Not the Other Way Around

At its core, service is about people. The best businesses understand that **technology exists to enhance human experiences, not replace them.** The moment businesses prioritize automation over connection, they risk turning service into a mere transaction—one that lacks warmth, empathy, and the ability to create lasting relationships.

The real winners in the future of service will be those who use AI **not as a shield between them and their customers but as a bridge.** AI should handle the repetitive, the mundane, and the routine, allowing humans to focus on what they do best: building trust, solving complex problems, and creating exceptional experiences. When used correctly, AI doesn't remove the human element—it strengthens it.

The businesses that will stand the test of time are the ones that never forget what service is truly about. Customers don't just remember what was done for them; they remember how they were made to feel. The future belongs to companies that embrace AI, not as a way to eliminate people but as a way to elevate them.

Delivering Exceptional Service in a Call Center

The Unique Challenges of Call Center Service

Unlike in-person interactions, call center employees do not have the advantage of body language, facial expressions, or physical gestures to create rapport with customers. This makes it even more essential to master verbal communication, tone, and problem-solving skills to ensure every caller feels heard, valued, and assisted in the best possible way.

In a highly competitive landscape, customer service is not just about answering questions—it's about making the caller feel that no other company understands them better. Businesses that invest in superior call center training create loyal customers who feel connected to the brand, even without face-to-face interactions.

Core Elements of Exceptional Call Center Service

1. **Active Listening**
   - Listen without interruptions.

- Use verbal nods (e.g., "I understand," "That makes sense," "I hear you").
- Paraphrase concerns to ensure understanding.

2. **Empathy and Emotional Intelligence**
- Recognize frustration or concerns and acknowledge them.
- Avoid robotic responses—tailor communication to the customer's emotions.
- Mirror tone and language appropriately.

3. **Tone and Pacing Mastery**
- Use a warm, welcoming tone.
- Adjust speed—too fast can overwhelm, too slow can frustrate.
- Avoid sounding scripted; be conversational.

4. **Clarity**
- Speak clearly and avoid jargon.
- Get to the point while maintaining warmth.
- Summarize action steps concisely.

5. **Personalization**
- Use the customer's name frequently but naturally.
- Reference previous interactions to show consistency.
- Tailor solutions to the individual rather than offering generic responses.

Innovative Ways to Make Your Call Center Service Stand Out

1. **Proactive Problem-Solving**
- Instead of waiting for complaints, anticipate needs and provide solutions before they escalate.
- Offer alternatives if a requested solution is unavailable.

2. **Follow-Up Calls and Check-Ins**
- A quick follow-up call to check satisfaction adds a personal touch.
- Even an automated message showing appreciation can leave a positive impression.

3. **Surprise and Delight**
- Empower agents to issue small goodwill gestures (discounts, extended warranties, and complimentary services) when a problem arises.
- Unexpected kindness fosters loyalty.

4. **Use of Storytelling**
   - A well-told example of how another customer benefited from a service or product builds trust.
   - Stories make interactions more engaging and relatable.
5. **Voice Smile Technique**
   - Smiling while speaking enhances vocal warmth.
   - Customers can detect positivity through vocal tone alone.

The Power of Words in Call Center Excellence

Since words are the only tool available, their selection is crucial. Some key points:

- **Avoid Negative Language**—Instead of saying "I can't do that," say, "Here's what I can do."
- **Use Positive Reinforcements**—"I'd be happy to assist you with that."
- **Mirror Customer Language**—This creates a sense of familiarity and connection.

Why Call Center Service Must Be Tailored to the Brand

Every company has different values, offerings, and customer expectations. Training must be customized to align with:

- **Company mission and culture**
- **Industry-specific needs**
- **Customer demographic expectations**

A well-trained call center representative is more than a voice—they are a brand ambassador who creates lasting loyalty.

PART 4

The Future of Service

The future of service isn't about faster transactions—it's about deeper connections. As technology evolves, the businesses that thrive will be the ones that balance efficiency with empathy, automation with authenticity, and convenience with genuine care.

CHAPTER 12

Service Training as an Investment, Not an Expense

Why a Business Should Make Service Training Paramount

Service training is not just an afterthought—it is the foundation upon which great businesses are built. It influences customer loyalty, brand reputation, team morale, and, ultimately, the bottom line. When businesses prioritize service training, they create environments where customers feel valued, employees feel empowered, and success becomes a sustainable reality.

Investing in service training ensures that employees are well-equipped to handle various customer interactions, from standard transactions to unique challenges. When team members understand the shades of excellent service, they contribute to building a culture of excellence that fosters customer retention and positive word-of-mouth marketing.

The Role of Service in Brand Differentiation

In competitive industries, service quality often distinguishes one brand from another. Products and prices can be replicated, but exceptional service is difficult to duplicate. Businesses that emphasize service training ensure that customers receive consistent, high-quality interactions that create lasting impressions.

Service Training and Employee Morale

Employees who receive comprehensive service training are more confident in their roles, leading to increased job satisfaction and lower turnover rates. When team members feel equipped to handle customer needs effectively, they develop a sense of pride in their work, which translates into better service delivery.

Service as an Experience

Service is not merely about completing a transaction—it is about creating an experience. Businesses that focus on service training teach employees how to transform routine interactions into memorable moments. This involves mastering skills such as eye contact, tone of voice, body language, and genuine empathy.

Addressing Difficult Customer Interactions

No business is immune to difficult customer situations, but well-trained employees can turn challenges into opportunities. Service training equips the team with the skills to manage complaints gracefully, de-escalate tense situations, and find solutions that leave customers feeling heard and valued.

Building a Loyal Customer Base

Loyalty is built on trust, and trust is built through consistent, high-quality service. Customers who experience outstanding service are more likely to return, recommend the business to others, and develop a long-term relationship with the brand. Service training ensures that every customer interaction reinforces this trust.

Customers appreciate when businesses go the extra mile to personalize their experience. Simple gestures, such as using a customer's name, remembering their preferences, and following up with thoughtful gestures, can have a profound impact. Service training teaches employees how to integrate personalization into their interactions naturally and effectively.

Internal Service: The Backbone of External Service

Great service doesn't start with customers—it starts within the team. A company that prioritizes internal service fosters a culture of respect, collaboration, and mutual support among employees. When team members treat each other with the same level of service expected for customers, the overall service quality improves.

Service Training as an Investment, Not an Expense

Some businesses view service training as a cost rather than an investment. However, the long-term benefits—higher customer retention, increased sales, and enhanced brand reputation—far outweigh the initial investment. Companies that consistently train their team and revisit this training in service excellence reap substantial financial and cultural rewards.

Making Service Training Paramount

Service is the heartbeat of any successful business. When businesses commit to making service training a top priority, they cultivate environments where customers feel valued, employees are engaged, and growth becomes inevitable. By embedding service excellence into the company culture, businesses can ensure long-term success and sustainability.

Service Is Not a Half-Hour Lesson

In too many businesses, service training is treated like a one-off task—something to "tick off" during onboarding or squeezed into a half-hour huddle before a shift. But real service—**memorable, human, relationship-building service**—doesn't come from a single session, a printed script, or a training video. It comes from **culture**, consistency, and commitment.

> Service is not a half-hour lesson.
> It's a living value, expressed in a thousand different ways every day.
> It's something we *model*, not just *mention*.

The Myth of the Quick Fix

When teams are told to "deliver great service" but only given a handful of rushed instructions, we create a dangerous gap: **expectation without**

foundation. It's like handing someone a musical instrument and expecting them to play beautifully after a few chords.

A half-hour can teach you how to smile.
But it won't teach you *why* smiling matters.
It might cover what to say, but not *how to listen*.
It can introduce a system, but not *build a standard*.
True service excellence is not learned.
It's absorbed. It's practiced. It's lived.

Culture over Crash Courses

The best service teams in the world don't rely on one-off lessons. They build service into **daily habits, rituals, and conversations**. It's in the way leaders speak to staff. It's in the debriefs, the celebrations, and the storytelling after a great customer moment.

If a company only talks about service during training, it stays a *task*.
When a company talks about service every day, it becomes a *truth*.
To embed service, we must **integrate it**:

- In team meetings: Celebrate the moments that made a difference.
- In performance feedback: Recognize *how* the job was done, not just *what* was done.
- In leadership behavior: Model respect, empathy, and consistency.
- In recruitment: Hire people who care, not just those who comply.

Service Is Muscle Memory

Like any skill, service sharpens with repetition. It gets better when you:

- Reflect on what worked and what didn't.
- Watch how others handle difficult moments.
- Try again when you miss the mark.
- Hear real stories, not hypothetical ones.

Half-hour lessons might give your team the "what."

But only ongoing coaching, culture, and care will give them the "why," the "how," and the *heart*.

The Leadership Challenge

As leaders, it's tempting to believe service can be solved quickly. But that's like watering a plant once and expecting it to bloom forever. To create a service-driven environment, you have to:

- Show up every day with intention.
- Catch people doing it right.
- Talk about service like it matters—because it does.

You're not just delivering training.

You're creating **a standard, a rhythm, and a story** your team becomes part of.

A Lifelong Lesson

Service is a lifelong lesson, not a line in a manual. It's not about perfection—it's about **presence**. About noticing people. Listening deeply and caring enough to go one step further.

And that kind of service?
It's not taught in a half-hour.
It's taught in moments.
It's taught in culture.
It's taught by example.

Because when service becomes who we are—not just what we do—it transforms our teams, our businesses, and the lives of every customer we meet. And that's something no short training can ever replace.

Hospitality Beyond Food Service

Hospitality is not just about food service; it's about creating an atmosphere where people feel at home. True hospitality is about making people feel welcomed, understood, and valued—whether in a café, a retail store, a hotel, or even a corporate setting. The businesses that master this art build unwavering customer loyalty.

Think of the places you love returning to. It's not just about the product or service—it's the feeling you get when you walk in. Do the staff remember you? Do they greet you warmly? Do they create an environment where you feel comfortable and appreciated? These factors make all the difference in retaining customers.

When a business fosters a culture of genuine hospitality, customer retention stops being a concern. Customers don't just return because they need a product; they return because of how the experience makes them feel. Whether you're a barista, a sales associate, or a manager, mastering the feeling of welcoming people as if they were stepping into their own homes can elevate your service and set you apart from competitors.

What Do the Customers See?

When you walk into a business, what is the first thing you notice? Is it the warm, inviting atmosphere, the friendly team members greeting you with a smile, or is it something entirely different—a cluttered space, employees too busy to acknowledge your presence, or an environment that feels cold and unwelcoming? The way a customer perceives a business in their first moments of arrival shapes their entire experience, and, therefore, as service professionals, it is our responsibility to ensure that what they see aligns with what we want them to feel.

Seeing Through the Customer's Eyes

One of the most powerful exercises I have ever conducted in team training is taking my team outside and asking them to observe everything as if they were a customer visiting for the first time. I would strategically place subtle indicators of neglect—rubbish on the ground, half-eaten meals left on tables, chairs slightly askew, a team member deliberately avoiding eye contact, and another checking their watch repeatedly. Then, I would gather my team back inside and ask, "What did you see?"

At first, many would only pick up on the obvious—paper on the floor, an abandoned coffee cup. But after repeating the exercise and prompting them to think deeper, they would begin to recognize how body language, engagement, and the overall environment affect customer perception. It was always a moment of awakening.

Customers do not enter a business thinking about how hard the team is working behind the scenes or how many hours went into perfecting the menu, displays, or service scripts. What they see and experience in the moment is all that matters to them. That means we must be hyper-aware of how our space and team present themselves at every given second.

Imagine walking into a café where the team are so engrossed in their tasks that no one looks up to greet you. You notice a wobbly table near the entrance, crumbs on an otherwise empty chair, and a display case with smudged glass. These are small details, but they accumulate into an impression of neglect. Conversely, a customer entering a well-kept, welcoming space where the team acknowledge them instantly, everything is clean and in place, and the atmosphere feels warm and engaging will walk away feeling valued and appreciated.

Creating a Visually Inviting Space

Every business has a physical presence that contributes to the overall customer experience. Here are a few key aspects to consider:

1. **Cleanliness and Order:**
   - Floors, tables, counters, and seating areas should always be pristine. A single sticky table or a chair covered in crumbs can deter a customer.
   - Ensure that rubbish bins are not overflowing and that common areas are always tidy.
   - Walk around your business regularly to see if anything looks out of place or unkempt.
2. **Team Presence and Engagement:**
   - Are employees making eye contact and acknowledging customers as they enter?
   - Are staff members engaged and approachable, or are they distracted by their tasks?
   - Are body language and facial expressions warm and inviting?

3. **Merchandising and Visibility:**
   - Are your best-selling items in a position of prominence?
   - Are promotional materials displayed in a way that draws attention without feeling cluttered?
   - Are there items that could be repositioned for better visibility?
4. **Ambience and Atmosphere:**
   - Is the lighting too dim or too harsh?
   - Does the background music complement the setting or overpower conversations?
   - Is the temperature comfortable for guests?

Before service begins, every team member should take a moment to walk through the space as if they were a customer. This should be a daily practice—an opportunity to see things from a fresh perspective. Small changes, like repositioning a misplaced chair or wiping down a menu, can have a massive impact on a guest's perception.

Encouraging the team to adopt this mindset helps create a culture of attentiveness and accountability. When everyone is invested in ensuring that customers see nothing but excellence, the business thrives.

Training the Team to See What Customers See

Many employees become so immersed in their routine that they stop noticing their surroundings. Training them to develop a customer's perspective requires intentional coaching.

Here's how to instill this habit:

1. **Conduct Regular Walkthroughs:**
   - Assign team members to different areas of the business and ask them to assess their spaces.
   - Have a daily checklist of things to inspect before opening and throughout the shift.
2. **Role-Reversal Exercises:**
   - Allow the team to experience the business as a customer—have them order a meal, sit at different tables, or use the restrooms to ensure they understand what guests experience.

3. **Encourage Feedback from Customers:**
   ○ Engage with guests and ask about their experience—what stood out, what could be improved.
   ○ Read online reviews and discuss them with the team to identify patterns.
4. **Lead by Example:**
   ○ If leadership takes the time to see the space through the customers' eyes, employees will follow suit.
   ○ Managers should demonstrate how to spot and correct minor issues before they become noticeable to customers.

Customers are making micro-assessments the moment they enter a business. Their perception is influenced by countless small cues, whether they consciously register them or not. A well-kept environment signals care, professionalism, and high standards. A chaotic or neglected space, even in minor ways, signals indifference and lack of attention.

By controlling what customers see, businesses control how they feel. And how they feel determines whether they return, recommend, or never come back.

At the end of the day, we must step back and ask ourselves, "What do our customers see?" If it's anything less than an inviting, professional, and well-run operation, then changes need to be made. The businesses that master this art will stand out because service is more than just what we do—it's the environment, the atmosphere, and the little details that show customers they are valued.

Being able to see through the customer's eyes is not just a skill; it is a necessity. And when a business truly understands this, it will always be one step ahead of the competition.

Designing a Service Training Program That Builds Brand Loyalty and Creates Service Superstars

Customer service is the backbone of any successful business. A well-trained service team is the difference between a one-time transaction and a lifelong customer. While many companies acknowledge the importance of customer service, far too many treat training as an afterthought—a rushed, 30-minute session that barely scratches the surface.

This approach is a mistake. Exceptional customer service is not just about smiling and being polite; it is about creating a holistic experience that keeps customers coming back. To achieve this, businesses must invest in comprehensive, tailored service training programs that align with their company values and provide employees with the tools, confidence, and mindset to excel.

Why Customer Service Training Must Be Tailored to Each Business

Not all businesses are the same, and a one-size-fits-all approach to service training is ineffective. Every company has unique values, brand promises, and customer expectations.

1. **Reinforcing Company Values**
   Your customer service team is the frontline representation of your brand. If they do not embody your company's values, your brand identity weakens. A tailored training program should include:
   - The company's mission and vision
   - Brand voice and tone
   - Core values and how they translate into service interactions
   - The customer experience expectations specific to your industry
     For example, a luxury retail brand requires a different level of service training than a fast-paced coffee shop. The key is to ensure employees understand how their service directly impacts brand perception.

2. **Meeting Customer Expectations**
   Different industries and businesses have unique customer expectations. A five-star hotel guest expects personalized service and attention to detail, whereas a quick-service restaurant customer values speed and efficiency. Training should cover:
   - Common customer expectations in the industry
   - Industry-specific service etiquette
   - How to exceed customer expectations

When training is tailored to meet these needs, employees can deliver service that resonates with customers and creates a memorable experience.

Why Service Training Needs to Be More Than a 30-Minute Session

Many businesses make the mistake of reducing customer service training to a brief, generic session. But great service cannot be learned in half-an-hour. A comprehensive training program ensures that employees are equipped with the skills and mindset to consistently provide exceptional service.

1. **Service Excellence Requires Skill Development**
   Service is not just about being welcoming—it is a skill that requires practice and refinement. Proper training should cover:
   - **Active Listening**: Understanding customer needs beyond what they say
   - **Emotional Intelligence**: Recognizing and managing customer emotions
   - **Problem-solving**: Handling complaints and unexpected situations effectively
   - **Communication Skills**: Ensuring clarity and professionalism in every interaction

2. **Handling Challenges with Confidence**
   Customers do not always arrive in a good mood. A well-trained service professional knows how to de-escalate tense situations, turn around negative experiences, and handle service delays effectively. Training should include:
   - Conflict-resolution techniques
   - Role-playing complex customer interactions
   - Strategies for keeping customers informed during delays
   - Techniques for maintaining composure under pressure
     When employees are prepared for difficult situations, they can turn potential complaints into moments of exceptional service.

3. **Creating Long-Term Customer Loyalty**
   Customer loyalty is not built through a single positive interaction; it is the result of **consistency**. A strong training program ensures

that every team member is aligned in their approach, creating a seamless and repeatable customer experience. Training should cover:

- ○ The psychology of customer loyalty
- ○ How to personalize service interactions
- ○ Strategies for building emotional connections with customers
- ○ The role of follow-ups in maintaining relationships

When employees understand the long-term impact of their service, they become more invested in delivering excellence.

The Service Superstar: Why Training Matters

A well-trained service professional is more than just an approachable employee; they are a **brand ambassador** who influences customer perception and loyalty. Here's what separates a service superstar from an average employee:

1. **They Keep Customers Coming Back**

   Customers return not just because of a product but because of the experience created by the service team. A superstar:
   - ○ Makes customers feel valued and appreciated
   - ○ Remembers customer preferences and personal details
   - ○ Anticipates needs before the customer expresses them
   - ○ Creates a feeling that the customer is a VIP

2. **They Handle Issues Effectively**

   No business is perfect; delays, mistakes, and challenges will occur. A well-trained service professional knows how to turn these moments into opportunities for loyalty by:
   - ○ Communicating openly and honestly about delays
   - ○ Offering solutions before customers need to ask
   - ○ Apologizing with sincerity and making things right

3. **They Build Brand Ambassadors**

   Satisfied customers do not just return—they advocate for the business. A service superstar creates such a strong emotional connection that customers:
   - ○ Recommend the business to friends and family.

- Leave positive reviews and testimonials.
- Choose the business over competitors, even when given alternatives.

What a Comprehensive Service Training Program Should Include

A strong service training program is not a single session but an ongoing process. Here's what it should include:

1. **Onboarding Training**
   The foundation of great service starts on Day 1. New employees should receive:
   - An introduction to company values and service expectations
   - Basic customer service skills and etiquette
   - Hands-on training with real-world scenarios

2. **Ongoing Skill Development**
   Service excellence is an ongoing commitment. Training should not stop after onboarding but should be reinforced through:
   - Monthly workshops on advanced service techniques
   - Peer coaching and mentorship programs
   - Continuous learning through real-life service examples

3. **Leadership Development**
   Great service comes from the top down. Businesses should invest in training leaders to:
   - Set the standard for service excellence.
   - Coach and mentor team members.
   - Handle escalated customer service situations.

4. **Real-World Simulations**
   The best way to learn service excellence is through practice. Training should include:
   - Role-playing exercises to practice customer interactions
   - Programs for objective feedback
   - Team challenges focused on exceeding customer expectations

5. **Measuring and Rewarding Excellence**
   To reinforce great service, businesses should:
   - Track customer feedback and service performance metrics.

- Recognize and reward outstanding service efforts.
- Use customer stories to highlight the impact of exceptional service.

Investing in service training is not an expense; it is an investment in long-term business success. A well-trained service team creates loyalty, drives revenue, and turns customers into lifelong brand ambassadors.

If businesses want to thrive, they must prioritize customer service training beyond a 30-minute session. They must make it a **core part of their culture** and ensure that every employee is equipped to create exceptional customer experiences. Because at the end of the day, it is not just about selling a product or a service—it is about creating relationships that last.

A well-trained service superstar is the greatest asset a business can have. They are the ones who keep customers coming back, who handle challenges with grace, and who turn everyday transactions into unforgettable experiences.

The question is not whether businesses can afford to invest in training. The real question is—can they afford not to?

The Power of a Service Training Program and the Psychology Behind Signing a Declaration

Many businesses limit customer service training to basic role-playing and transaction handling. While this may teach employees how to process orders or respond to inquiries, it does not equip them to create a service culture that fosters true customer loyalty.

Core Areas of a Strong Service Training Program

1. **Front-of-House (FOH) Training**
   - Greeting customers warmly upon arrival
   - Recognizing regular customers and building rapport
   - Upselling and adding value through genuine recommendations
   - Handling service issues professionally and proactively

2. **Back-of-House (BOH) Training**
   - Ensuring seamless operations to avoid service delays
   - Communicating with FOH staff effectively
   - Maintaining hygiene and safety standards to protect the brand's reputation
3. **Office and Support Staff Training**
   - Consistency in communication across all customer touchpoints
   - Handling inquiries via e-mail, social media, and calls professionally
   - Aligning messaging to reinforce the company's service philosophy

The Role of the Service Training Declaration

At the end of every training module, employees sign a declaration confirming:

- They have received and understood the service training.
- They acknowledge their role in delivering exceptional service.
- They recognize their responsibility to ensure the business is known for excellence.

The Psychology Behind Signing a Declaration

1. **Commitment and Accountability**
   - Psychologically, signing a document strengthens commitment.
   - Employees take ownership of their service role.
2. **Purpose and Reinforcement**
   - Reaffirming their purpose makes employees feel valued and integral to the company's success.
3. **Elevated Sense of Responsibility**
   - Seeing their name on a document creates a tangible link between their performance and the company's reputation.
4. **Building a Service-Driven Culture**
   - Reinforces that service excellence is a core business pillar, not an afterthought.

Why Training Must Be More Than a 30-Minute Session

Short training sessions often fail to instill service excellence because:

- Employees don't have time to absorb or practice key concepts.
- There's no reinforcement or follow-up on lessons learned.
- It minimizes the importance of service in overall business success.

Service training is the foundation of a successful business. Whether in a call center, a customer-facing role, or a back-office position, well-trained employees make the difference between a company that survives and a company that thrives.

Investing in thorough training programs, reinforcing them with a service declaration, and ensuring employees feel a personal commitment to excellence transforms customer service from a task into a defining brand experience. When employees truly understand their role in making customers feel valued, they create loyal brand advocates—one exceptional interaction at a time.

Bridging B2B and B2C: How This Book Serves Both Sides of the Customer Relationship

As you've explored throughout this book, meaningful customer service is about far more than transactions—it's about human connection, trust, and the moments that turn everyday interactions into lasting loyalty.

Now, as we near the close of this journey, it's important to reflect on how these principles apply across two seemingly different landscapes: **B2B (business-to-business)** and **B2C (business-to-consumer)**. While the dynamics may differ, the essence remains the same: **people doing business with people**.

This book is not just for retailers, hospitality workers, or those on the front lines of B2C service. It is just as relevant to those working in B2B environments, where relationships are longer-term, more complex, and often deeply personal in different ways.

For B2B: Deep Trust, Long-Term Relationships

In the B2B world, clients are partners. Service excellence here isn't about speed or volume—it's about **depth, trust, and consistency** over time.

By now, you've seen how going beyond the basics—through emotional connection, proactive support, and tailored service—creates loyalty. These same practices build strong B2B relationships that can span years or decades.

> **This book empowers B2B professionals to:**
> - **Anticipate client needs** by deeply understanding their business goals.
> - **Strengthen emotional loyalty**—because even the most data-driven decision makers are still human.
> - **Tailor service delivery** for each client, showing that their success is your priority.
> - **View every interaction as a relationship touchpoint**, not just a contract checkpoint.

For B2C: Emotional Impact in Every Interaction

On the B2C side, service is often fast-paced and emotionally charged. Customers want to be seen, heard, and valued—immediately. Loyalty in this space is won (and lost) in seconds, and moments matter.

> **This book helps B2C businesses:**
> - **Deliver emotional loyalty**, not just rewards programs.
> - **Create memorable, feel-good experiences** that stick.
> - **Listen to understand**, not just to respond.
> - **Exceed expectations** with small, thoughtful moments that become stories customers tell.

What They Have in Common

By now, one truth should be clear: **The label—B2B or B2C—doesn't matter as much as the relationship behind it**. Both demand empathy, attentiveness, and a genuine desire to serve.

Whether you're navigating the nuances of a long-term corporate contract or making someone's day with a latte and a smile, the same principles apply:

- Be present.
- Be proactive.
- Be human.

That's the heart of exceptional service. That's how loyalty is built, no matter the business model.

You've now seen how to go beyond transactions. You've reflected on kindness, empathy, and what it means to be truly customer-led. So, whether your next move is nurturing a business partnership or delighting a walk-in customer, let these principles guide you.

This book is your roadmap to stronger relationships, regardless of what your customer looks like. Because in the end, **we're all in the business of people.**

CHAPTER 13

An Ode to Change

As the cost of living rises, so do customers' expectations. Every dollar a customer spends is hard-earned, and, in return, they expect not just a product but an experience—a service that makes them feel valued. Businesses that understand this fundamental shift will rise above their competition.

We have explored the power of a warm welcome, the impact of eye contact, the art of deep listening, and the role of empathy in creating an exceptional service experience. But now, it is time to bring it all together. Service is no longer just a bonus; it is the defining factor that determines whether a business thrives or struggles.

In an era where customers have endless choices, their loyalty is earned through authentic connections and consistently exceptional experiences. The businesses that understand this—that train their teams not just in technical skills but also in the human elements of service—will be the ones that endure.

True service is about creating an environment where customers feel seen, heard, and appreciated. It is about ensuring that each interaction, no matter how small, reinforces their decision to choose your business over another.

The businesses that invest in service training recognize that it is not an expense—it is an investment in longevity, reputation, and success. Those who fail to do so will be left behind, as customers gravitate toward businesses that not only meet but also exceed their expectations.

Service excellence is a great differentiator. It is what transforms first-time visitors into loyal customers and, in turn, loyal customers into brand advocates. It is what turns a simple transaction into a memorable experience.

Now, as we conclude this journey, the question is no longer whether service matters—it is how committed you are to delivering it at the highest level. Will your business rise to the challenge? Will you embrace the opportunity to redefine service in your industry?

Change is inevitable, but the businesses that welcome it, adapt to it, and innovate through it will not just survive; they will lead the way.

This is your moment. This is your opportunity. The future of service is in your hands.

Be the Change in Hospitality

Hospitality is more than just a job or a transaction—it's a **human experience**. Every interaction you have with a customer is a moment of impact. A moment to create warmth, trust, and a sense of belonging. A moment to **turn a routine visit into a lasting memory**.

You are not just serving food, making coffee, or checking guests into a room—you are **welcoming people into your space, into your care, into your world**. Whether you are a business owner shaping the culture of your team or a frontline team member delivering service every day, **you are the difference** between an ordinary visit and an extraordinary one.

It's easy to think that change must come from the top. That someone else—management, corporate, and the industry as a whole—needs to set the standard. But real change happens **where the guest experience begins**: with you.

- If you lead a business, **set the example**. Create a culture where service is not just an expectation but, in fact, a passion.
- If you are a manager, **inspire your team**. Show them that every small action matters and that each role in the team has value.
- If you are on the front line, **own your impact**. Take pride in how you make people feel.

The Magic of Hospitality Is in the Little Things

Guests may not always remember what they ordered, but they will remember how you made them **feel**. They will remember the warmth in your welcome, the care in your service, and the small details that made their experience feel personal.

Hospitality is an **art**—one that requires heart, effort, and intention. It is built in the moments where you:

- Greet a guest like an old friend.
- Remember their name and their favorite drink.
- Go out of your way to make them feel valued.
- Anticipate their needs before they even have to ask.
- Take ownership of their experience from start to finish.

At the end of the day, **hospitality is about people**. Your ability to connect, to care, and to create a sense of home is what sets you apart. Whether you work in a small café, a luxury hotel, or a bustling restaurant, your impact matters. **You are the heart of hospitality.**

So go forward with intention. Lead the change. **Be the reason someone leaves with a smile—and comes back again and again.**

Great service isn't just about what you do. **It's about how you make people feel.**

Now, it's your turn to create the magic.

Be the Reason Someone Comes Back

References

Bater, D. (n.d.). *Why Customers Stop Buying*. Retrieved July 7, 2025, from https://davidbater.com/why-customers-stop-buying/.

Gallace, A., and Spence, C. (2010). "The Science of Interpersonal Touch: An Overview." *Neuroscience & Biobehavioral Reviews* 34(2): 246–259. https://doi.org/10.1016/j.neubiorev.2008.10.004.

Lencioni, P. (2002). *The Five Dysfunctions of a Team: A Leadership Fable*. Jossey-Bass.

Magids, S., A. Zorfas, and D. Leemon. 2015. "The New Science of Customer Emotions." *Harvard Business Review*, November. https://hbr.org/2015/11/the-new-science-of-customer-emotions.

Montague, E., Chen, P., Xu, J., Chewning, B., and Barrett, B. (2013). "Nonverbal Interpersonal Interactions in Clinical Encounters and Patient Perceptions of Empathy." *Journal of Participatory Medicine* 5: e33. https://participatorymedicine.org/journal/evidence/research/2013/08/14/nonverbal-interpersonal-interactions-in-clinical-encounters-and-patient-perceptions-of-empathy/.

Pezdek, K., and R. M. Eddy. 2001. "Impressions of Service Providers: The Role of Affective Expectations in Memory for Service Encounters." *Journal of Applied Psychology*.

About the Author

Jennard Rose has spent her career in service leadership, transforming underperforming businesses by building high-performing, customer-first teams. She's trained hundreds in the real-world art of delivering unforgettable service that drives loyalty, increases sales, and leaves a lasting impression.

Index

www.ingramcontent.com/pod-product-compliance
Lightning Source LLC
Chambersburg PA
CBHW061306220326
41599CB00026B/4750